The Scarlet Thread

A Book of Poems by

Lucy Wall

To Hazel,

May you be blessed
through these poems. With love
in Christ,

Lucy x

25·06·22

ISBN: 978-1-57821-817-2

I would like to thank my family and friends who have encouraged me throughout the years to keep writing and keep sharing what my Saviour puts on my heart. Thank you to everyone who has used a poem in their home group, at Church, as a tool while witnessing to others or during a special life event. You really are an answer to my prayer that the poems wouldn't sit doing nothing and instead be used for God's glory and to serve His purposes!

Special thanks has to go to my wonderful Mum who is normally the first to hear a new poem! Thanks for all the time you take to listen to and proof-read each one Mum. Your constant encouragement, input and words of wisdom are invaluable to me.

Thank you to my creative husband Jan whose music and songs have often been an inspiration to me. The hours we've spent walking laps around St James' Park while bouncing ideas off each other are precious to me. I imagine the trees could quote some Bible verses by now!

Of course my biggest thanks goes to my Lord and Saviour Jesus Christ. To the God who makes the impossible possible, may the glory always be Yours.

Table of Contents

INTRODUCTION

A warm welcome to you dear reader and I pray my book of poetry can be a blessing in your life. This is my first book to be published so I think I should introduce myself a little! My name is Lucy Wall and I'm originally from Motherwell in Scotland where I grew up with my sister Ashley and my Mum and Dad. I now live in London with my husband Jan and we've been married since 2009.

I moved to London after finishing High School and spent three years training on a Musical Theatre course at Arts Educational Schools in Chiswick. After graduating I went on a U.K and International tour with the show "Oh! What A Night" where I played the lead role "Cat." I then toured with the show "Chicago" playing the role of "Kitty" and understudying the leading characters "Velma Kelly" and "Mamma Morton."

In 2005 I started my first West End job as an ensemble member in the show "Fame" and understudied the roles "Carmen," "Miss Bell" and "Mabel" before going on to play the lead role of "Carmen" full time. In 2006 I then went back into "Chicago," this time in the West End and playing the character "June." In 2007 I joined the West End cast of "Mamma Mia" and played the role of "Ali." I was also given the wonderful opportunity of promoting the show in places such as Kuala Lumpur, Paris, Milan and Belgium.

In 2009 I became part of the original West End cast of "Legally Blonde." I performed as a swing for the first two years which meant I covered eight people and subsequently was kept very busy indeed, sometimes playing several people's characters within the same show!

It was a wonderful experience being part of an original production and we had the honour of winning several awards in our first year alone, one of them even being an Olivier! In October 2011 I took on the character of "Serena" full time and finished playing this role when the show closed in April 2012.

In July of the same year I joined the West End Show "Matilda" playing the role of "The Acrobat" and understudying the lead roles of "Mrs Phelps" and "Miss Honey." I went on to work on a new theatre project called "Kingmaker" in 2015 which took a satirical look at the world of politics. I then enjoyed a U.K and Ireland tour in late 2017 leading into 2018, playing the role of "Sister Berthe" and understudying "Baroness Elsa" in the well known musical "The Sound of Music."

In the Autumn of 2018, eleven years after appearing in the show in the West End I was given the chance to promote the film "Mamma Mia" in an immersive performance in Abu Dhabi, then also "Mamma Mia 2" in Spring 2019. This time I played one of the lead roles "Tanya" and was over the moon to be back having some more "Mamma Mia" fun!

The reason for this book however is not for the performer in me but rather the hopeful poet! I enjoyed writing poetry as a young girl but forgot about it for many years of my life. It wasn't until I committed my life to Jesus Christ in 2006 that I was reminded by Him that writing was something I liked to do. The difference now however was that I found myself writing about Jesus and feeling inspired by the different events that He allows into my life. This is very much in line with the inspiration for the title of my book.

In the Bible, a scarlet thread physically appears several times. We see it in Genesis 38 at the birth of the twin boys of Judah and Tamar, Exodus 26 in the fabric of the curtains in the Tabernacle and Joshua 2 during the story of Rahab. There is also the opinion that there is a symbolic scarlet thread running through the entirety of the Bible. It's said to be a picture of the blood of Jesus Christ, shed on the Cross to wash away sin.

We see the first example of this in Genesis when God Himself slaughtered an animal in order to cover the rebellious Adam and Eve with it's skin. Here we see the first picture of how the innocent had to die to cover the guilty, ultimately pointing to Christ's death on the Cross for us. Many allegorical pictures such as this appear throughout the Bible and this is what some Theologians refer to as "the scarlet thread."

Just as Christ's presence can be seen in this emblematic way, I feel that it's the same within the life of a believer. As I go through this life,

Jesus infiltrates and influences every aspect of it. His presence within my heart affects the way I view situations, make decisions and deal with the different circumstances that make up life's fabric. As I journey through different events in life I feel as if the Holy Spirit is the one who is weaving everything together and creating the picture of my life with Jesus as a constant, winding presence. I hope that my poetry reflects this and my desire is to use each poem to share the wonderful, soul-saving truth of the Gospel of Jesus Christ. I pray they can be used as tools to tell others of the incredible, often very natural ways God works within our hearts.

The poems cover many different topics and each comes with an introduction section that explains my inspiration on how I came to write it. I've placed the poems in the order in which I wrote them so that the progress of my faith throughout the years can be seen. The poems are written as separate entities however so they can be read in any order at all. I've also put their titles into categories on a separate page for anyone who may wish to find a poem that covers a particular subject. May these poems be used to comfort, encourage, guide, convict and ultimately bring glory to the wonderful name of Jesus! As I always pray before I share any poem, "Not a word from me Lord but all of You through me!" I think Ephesians 3:14-21 says it superbly,

"For this reason I bow my knees to the Father of our Lord Jesus Christ, from whom the whole family in heaven and earth is named, that He would grant you, according to the riches of His glory, to be strengthened with might through His Spirit in the inner man, that Christ may dwell in your hearts through faith; that you, being rooted and grounded in love, may be able to comprehend with all the saints what is the width and length and depth and height-to know the love of Christ which passes knowledge; that you may be filled with all the fullness of God. Now to Him who is able to do exceedingly abundantly above all that we ask or think, according to the power that works in us, to Him be glory in the church by Christ Jesus to all generations, forever and ever. Amen."

For audio and visual recordings of my poetry please go to www.lucywallpoetry.co.uk

THE NARROW AND WIDE GATES

INSPIRATION

"The Narrow And Wide Gates" is the first poem I wrote after giving my heart to Jesus in August 2006. I felt inspired to write it after reading Matthew 7:13-14 which reads,

"Enter through the narrow gate, for wide is the gate and broad is the road that leads to destruction and many enter through it. But narrow is the gate and narrow the road that leads to life and only a few find it."

Immediately after reading these verses I started to picture the two contrasting gates that Matthew describes. I began to write down what I could see in my mind's eye and as the poem developed I realised I was writing about the spiritual journey I had just been on as the Holy Spirit called my heart to follow Jesus and enter through the "Narrow Gate!"

I was just a few months old in the Lord when I wrote this poem so it isn't filled with Scriptures and Biblical references but it is full of symbolism. I used this to expose the seemingly harmless but deadly temptations of the devil and show how Jesus is the only One who truly leads to contentment, peace, joy and most importantly, life!

POEM

One day I wandered through the trees and found myself a gate.
"What paths will lie beyond these bars?" my thoughts did contemplate.
The shining, golden, gleaming front was pleasing to my eye.
"Whatever lies behind such beauty must be worth a try!"

I noticed then the looming doors had jewels down every side,
Encrusted treasures hidden deep within these gates so wide.
The gems began to dazzle me, blinking, full of promise
And whispering their songs so sweet, reciting "Come and join us!"

My eyes I could not tear away from these gates before me,
Hypnotised I stood and stared at this resplendent glory.
I noticed then there was no lock and no need for a key;
These gates were opened many times and very easily.

Transfixed was I and in a spell, no chance to run and hide.
Towards the gates my limbs were pulled, my feet began to glide.
As I approached the massive gates swung open without strain,
From deep within, melodic voices beckoning my name.

The scented air was filled with fragrance, wonderfully sweet.
Henceforth came creatures from the dark to welcome and to greet.
They reached for me with baleful grins, "Come with us!" they'd insist.
By now the tempting ways they had I found hard to resist.

I lost control of mind and movement, senses in a trance
As round and round into the dark I joined their merry dance.
Their machinations tricked my mind, I found this place delicious.
Obliviously unaware of plans or schemes pernicious.

They led me to a place so full of promises and dreams,
A myriad of swirling colour bursting at the seams!
Far behind those gates of gold I felt I found a place
Where one could do just as they please and never have to face

A reprimand or consequence, you had to pay no fee.
Yes all this came without a price, apparently for free.
So further on and deeper still I ventured in this land
Though deep recesses of my mind could hear a ticking hand.

Yet lustfully my eyes would bathe and drink in lustrous wonder
At lightening skies and diamond stars and looming clouds of thunder.
I found myself engulfed in petals, flowers crimson deep,
Soft as velvet to the touch like kisses in my sleep.

'Twas as I lay in false pretence warm feelings were enfolding
Then just like that within my gut, sensations so foreboding.
My eyes shot open, snapped awake, I came to realise,
Despite the promise this land held perhaps there was no prize.

I looked around and what had seemed at first so full of beauty
Was now a pallid, fetid place, full of sin and cruelty.
The acrid air, it filled my lungs poisoning my soul.
My every fibre suffering as evil took it's toll.

Surrounding me, the many eyes were staring, full of guile
And from the shadows they would watch and with a furtive smile.
So languidly I hauled myself and forced my legs to run
And just in time I realised this place was not such fun.

I tore through branches, weeds and vines, I had to find that gate
And get myself away from here before it was too late.
I felt my strength recovering as through the brush I'd hack.
I would not stop until I knew my self-control was back!

I found the path that was so wide, the gate lay up ahead.
I noticed then that from this side the gate was black and dead.
No glittering or promises enticing me to stay,
By now I knew of my mistake and fought to get away.

A mighty battle then commenced between my soul and body.
"How could these charms have kept me here?" I scolded my own folly.
I dragged my legs through air so dense like running through
thick liquid.
My muscles burned and weighed me down, my soul grew dim
and timid.

At last I reached the rotting gates and threw my weight upon them,
Bursting through my soul released from dark despair and mayhem.
My legs collapsed and there I lay, gasping on the ground.
So silently the gates slid shut without a single sound.

Trembling and in despair I tried to sit up straight
But could not bare to turn around and face that awful gate.
So all alone and very lost that no one heard my cries
And then I looked and looked again, could I believe my eyes?

The golden gate had markings now or did my eyes play tricks?
Upon the front a serpent sat with numbers "666."
My blood ran cold, I turned away, my throat let out a cry
Then in the midst of my despair a new thing caught my eye.

A gentle calm and quiet peace, it filled my very core.
I looked upon another gate, a slender, subtle door.
Made of wood and painted white, I saw this gate so humble.
I forced myself to stand up straight, my feet began to stumble.

Surrounded by the foliage, entwining convolution,
This gate was pure but most of all was free from sin's pollution.
No magnet force was pulling me, no hypnotising voice.
This time I staggered to the gate entirely by choice.

As I approached my soul grew strong, my heart lit like a candle.
On close inspection there I found the absence of a handle.
I raised my hand and pressed with force, 'twas then I felt quite shocked
To find this tiny, narrow gate was very firmly locked.

I knocked three times and called aloud then gave another nudge.
So in despair and quite perplexed at how it would not budge.
Frustration then possessed my heart, I fell down on my knees.
I clasped my hands and wept and prayed, "Just open for me, please!"

So as I sat besides myself, I felt quite at a loss
I noticed then upon the door the marking of a Cross.
A desperate longing filled my soul to see the other side.
"I need your help, O' mighty Lord" still on my knees I cried.

Face in my hands and sobbing hard, I felt my torment peak
Then just as I thought all was lost it opened with a creak.
So through my tears I looked ahead and saw a dazzling light
Peeking through in rays and beams so wonderfully bright.

I reached my hand in front of me, I felt I'd need a guide
To take my hand and comfort me and help me walk inside.
I felt a warm, assuring grip clasp round my trembling hand
And lovingly He raised me up, helping me to stand.

Step by step I made my way, guided to the door,
My beating heart had heard a call, a call I'd not ignore.
By now the door was open wide, the whiteness blinded me.
I closed my eyes as from now on I'd use my heart to see.

Already I could feel the joy that this new land would bring,
I felt renewed and born again like bluebells in the spring!
This time I walked with confidence and disappeared for good
Behind that gentle, quiet door of soft white paint and wood.

And as it shut my spirit soared, filled deep with joy and wealth.
All that was left among those trees? A shadow of myself.
Although I'd strayed and wandered far, my mind had tried to roam,
I know that now I'm through that gate I've found my way back home.

Scripture References

Jeremiah 29:12-13; John 8:32

COMPARISON TO A RUBY

INSPIRATION

In December 2006 I went home to Scotland to spend the festive season with my family. It was late one night during my time there when I was casually sifting through my Bible and I happened to come across Proverbs 31. I found it to be a very interesting chapter that spoke about a virtuous wife and some of the desirable qualities she might possess.

As a young, single woman at that time I couldn't really relate to the woman described in the passage although I certainly felt the description was something to aspire to if I ever did get married. What really got a hold of my thoughts however was verse ten which reads,

"A wife of noble character, who can find? She is worth far more than rubies."

I found myself thinking, "What a curious comparison to make, to compare a wife to a ruby!" I began to think about the different qualities that a wife might bring and some of the qualities a ruby might bring and then began to compare the two. It was these thoughts that inspired me to start writing "Comparison To A Ruby."

I've had the pleasure of sharing this poem at several weddings over the years and I pray it can be used to bless many couples as they begin their journey together as husband and wife!

POEM

Can you compare a wife to a ruby,
To it's wonderful crimson depths?
It's vision and form so sacred
With it's angles and shapes complex.

It's beauty will be eternal,
With this she cannot compete
But when has a man ever looked for
A *ruby* to make him complete?

It's face will always be ageless
And body hard as a nail
But she will be warm and gentle
With love that will never fail.

A ruby is priceless in value,
A thousand debts it'll pay.
But her love for *him* will be priceless,
A treasure he won't give away.

A ruby will never be faithful,
To rubies you cannot confide
But she can listen for hours,
His thoughts he won't have to hide.

A ruby is truly delightful!
A sparkling gem in the sand
But she will be his companion
To walk with through life, hand in hand.

She *could* try to be just as dazzling
And woo him with ruby red charms
But what could be more inviting
Than the tender embrace of her arms?

A ruby has elegant contours
With-holding it's secrets unknown
But loving this scarlet desire
Could turn any man's heart to stone.

For though he may lavish his interest
And compliment day after day,
His blandishments fall down unnoticed
For a ruby will never repay.

It never will share his emotion
Or whisper sweet nothings to him.
Inscrutably silent forever
And never inviting him in.

Impervious to his attention,
Content in it's own solitude.
One might think it vain and conceited
But a ruby can't feel, nor it should.

But *she's* formed of intricate levels,
Each one more intriguing than last.
He'll cherish each day spent beside her,
Together in future and past.

And though she may not be perfect
And sometimes fall victim to sin,
He'll search in his heart for forgiveness
For she'll do the same and for him.

There *is* a significant difference
Though both bring rewards he can reap
But once he has passed into Heaven,
A ruby he won't get to keep.

It *may* be his treasured possession,
He may place it's value so high
But it's earthly fulfilment is fleeting
And gone in the blink of an eye.

With her he can store all his treasure,
Investing his love 'til the end.
Devotion to her won't be wasted
For in Heaven he'll see her again!

Can you compare a wife to a ruby?
To a man could she be worth more?
He'll find when he meets his soul mate
He'll wonder how he'd lived before.

Scripture references

Ephesians 5:25-27; Proverbs 12:4

STILL IN MOULDING

INSPIRATION

"Still In Moulding" is the third poem I wrote after giving my life to Jesus. Unlike my first two poems I didn't receive my inspiration from any particular verse in the Bible but rather it came from what I felt the Lord was bringing out of my heart at the time.

It became apparent to me that at this point in my life I often found myself thinking about the fact that I was single. As I thought more deeply about this I began to consider what qualities I might now desire in a man and what kind of person I would consider could potentially be my husband.

As I began to write this poem it was really interesting for me to discover what I was now looking for in a spouse and there were certainly a few surprises there! The poem starts off with a very light-hearted, jovial tone and I had a lot of fun discovering what boxes my "Mr Right" would have to tick!

As I sat reading through my words and ideas for my unknown, mysterious "Mr Right" I started to think, "Hey this guy sounds great! I wish he was here now! Actually, why isn't he here now? Why am I single?"

This thought then lead me to dwell on the love of my Saviour and His sovereignty in my life. I began to meditate on His good and perfect judgements and how He knows what's best for me. The more I considered His flawless ways the more I realised that Jesus is in absolute control. I then rested in the knowledge that for as long as I was single, that was as long as I was meant to be single for! I knew that if it were better for me to be with someone then I would be! I had the desire in my heart to meet the right person but for some reason unknown to myself, God saw it better for me to be single at that time.

I then went on to consider how we meet people at appointed times in our lives and only when God allows us to, not a minute sooner, not a minute later. Whether the relationship is a friend, relative or future spouse, we meet them when God permits us to as all things work according to His perfect timing. Romans 8:28 certainly confirms this. I felt like God was moulding and shaping me on a daily basis into the woman that Jesus wanted me to be. Knowing that I wanted to be married to a godly man I didn't resent the thought of being slowly fashioned into a godly woman.

It was these thoughts that developed into the title "Still In Moulding" and gave me the second half of my poem. I had a peace in my heart that the Lord had a husband in store for me but I didn't know why I wasn't ready for him yet. I figured it could be for any number of reasons so I relinquished the desire to control this aspect of my life and gave it over to the Lord. What wonderful freedom and peace I found knowing I could completely trust in His perfect timing. With my eyes on Jesus I knew I could rest easy and leave the work to Him!

POEM

A question often in my mind, "Does "Mr Right" exist?"
Is there a man who'll tick each box on my extensive list?
What aspirations do I have when I envisage him?
His character or confidence that come from deep within.

I hope he's strong within his faith and feels a passion there.
He'll teach me things I never knew, this passion we will share.
His knowledge will run far and wide, at least, that's what I pray.
He'll also love to learn and listen to the things *I* say.

He'll have ambitions and ideas, have targets, goals and dreams.
He won't play games so juvenile, he'll say just what he means.
He knows his mind and what he likes, a grounded man he'll be.
He'll love to open up his life and make some room for me!

He'll share my humour, make me laugh, we'll have our "silly jokes."
Amuse our-selves for hours on end, I can't stand boring blokes!
A staid demeanour he won't possess, he's vivacious, fun and smart.
By being true to who he is, is how he'll steal my heart.

In honesty I don't imagine what his looks will be.
His features, face and colourings are just not up to me.
For me to plan minute details I think is not so clever.
He'll look the way he's *meant* to look, I'll love him so whatever.

We'll be a team, work as a pair, take turns to compromise.
Just knowing that he's mine to keep will give me butterflies.
He'll like to make a fuss of me, "the apple of his eye."
Be patient, bold and trustworthy and good at D.I.Y!

He doesn't need extravagance or riches to be mine
For opulence I do not seek, on me he'll spend his time.
Should he *insist* on spoiling me just to say "Love you!"
Leave little presents here or there, I guess that's alright too!

Well sounds like I know what I want and what I'm looking for
So why has "Mr Right" not yet come charging through my door?
I don't expect a "Superman" who flies at lightning speed
Or "Prince Charming" to whisk me off upon his noble steed.

The man for me will just be real, my love for him won't tire.
A man to share a lifetime with, a man I can admire.
I live a life salubrious and always law abiding
So why has he not turned up yet and why's he still in hiding?

Perhaps I'm just not old enough or need to change my look.
Maybe I need to travel more or teach myself to cook!
Perhaps I lack experience in matters of the heart
Or need more time to heal the wounds that make the tear ducts start.

I think the Lord is teaching me to put my trust in Him,
To set my focus Heavenward when fear and doubt creep in.
He's teaching me that in His Word is where I'll find the cure,
That perseverance makes me grow more spiritually mature.

It's when I'm ready that I know that he and I will meet.
Until that day I guess God's work in me is incomplete.
Whatever traits or qualities God feels I must possess
Or lessons learnt or knowledge stored, I don't yet have I guess.

I feel the Lord is moulding me with each new passing day,
Less of me and more of Him and walking in *His* way.
My thoughts are changing, views adjust, opinions take a turn.
The more I open up my heart the more I seem to learn.

The Lord knows how I need to be for "Mr Right" to fall
And knows what I will need in *him* for him to be *my* all.
Perhaps it's *him* who needs some work! Now there's a thought
that's new!
It isn't me who needs to grow, *he* needs a tweak or two!

These things will be part of the plan but deep inside I know,
It's when I'm least expecting him that "Mr Right" will show.
Who knows the time or place we'll meet, who knows the "when"
or "how."
If someone told me where he'd be I think I'd race there now!

But such details aren't mine to know for what will be will be.
"The future..." someone once described, "...is just not ours to see."
I *could* let anger take a hold, frustration make demands.
Instead I pray for quiet peace and leave it in *God's* hands.

For He's the one who knows me best and maps out my life's plan.
If this is in God's will for me I *know* I'll meet my man!
Until that day I trust the Lord will mould and shape my life.
He'll gently change me from a girl into a suited wife.

I know the man God has for me is more than worth the wait.
He'll be my friend and confidante. My husband. My soul-mate.
But why not now? Why make us wait when love could be unfolding?
I guess we're just not ready yet. I guess...we're still in moulding.

Scripture References

Psalm 37:4

Afterword

Needless to say, Jesus brought my husband along in His perfect time and I actually had the pleasure of sharing this poem with my guests on my own wedding day! By this time the Lord had used the poem mightily in my own life.

When things were developing between myself and Jan, I was chatting with my Mum one evening about whether he could be "Mr Right" or not. My Mum suggested that perhaps I should read my poem so I pulled it up on my laptop and began to read aloud. I only got a few verses through and then stopped. My Mum asked me why I had stopped reading and I replied, "Mum, this is a description of Jan!"

At the time of writing the poem I hadn't known Jan well at all. I knew of him as "the Pastor's son" at Church but I had barely spoken to him on more than a few occasions and our conversations had been very surface level. By the time I was reading the poem on that particular evening however I had gotten to know Jan over the course of about a year. Although I didn't know who I was describing at the time of writing, I realised that night as I sat with my Mum that the poem was actually about Jan.

God really spoke to my heart in that moment and showed me that not only was this the man He wanted as my husband but also this was the man that I wanted as my husband! Along with several other things such as reading Scriptures, godly counsel and lots of prayer, it was a huge confirmation to me that I could proceed with God's blessing. I guess you could say the rest is history!

Whenever I'm sharing this poem with others, especially young, single women, I always like to bring a focus around to the Scripture that I place at the end of this poem. As Psalm 37:4 reads,

"Delight yourself in the Lord and He will give you the desires of your heart."

I really felt that this was a lesson Jesus taught me during the two years before Jan came on the scene, the years I was "Still In Moulding" you might say! So often with that Scripture I think we like to jump in our minds to the last bit which says "He will give you the desires of your heart" and we think "Oh yes please! I like the sound of that!" Of course the key part however is the first bit which says "Delight yourself in the Lord!"

From my understanding of this verse and from what I've found to be true in my own life, the more we genuinely find our delight in God, the more content we will be in Him alone and the desires of our heart will be in line with what He desires for us. When we're in close communion with someone we connect intimately and are in sync with one another. It's the same in our relationship with Jesus. When we truly find our delight in Him our desires are submitted to God's will and we want what He wants for us. Our desires become one and the same and so it takes away any striving. Having this joy and peace in our lives is such a wonderful privilege as it takes away the need to fret over our future. Why would we fret? We have a sovereign God taking care of us!

A message I also like to share in line with this poem is that it's not about "finding a husband," not at all. It's about serving Jesus, trusting our desires to Him and going where He wants us to go in life. It's about each individual becoming the person that God wants them to be.

Jesus taught me that as a single Christian female I lacked absolutely nothing! God showed me that with Jesus we have everything we need and more because He is enough! It's Jesus who is our Husband first and foremost, Jesus is our Protector, our Provider, our Confidante and our constant Companion. He understands us entirely and will never let us down or leave us. I once heard it said that we should never try to make another person our Saviour. It's too much pressure to put on a flawed human being and they'll only let you down, no matter how much they may love you.

If we're looking for another person to complete us and make us feel whole then we're looking in the wrong place. It's Christ who completes us in ways no other human being ever could. When I started to get to grips with this truth I discovered such wonderful independence and contentment. That's not to say it was always easy, I certainly had some trials during this time. I had to dig deep into God's Word and remember His promises for me but I can honestly say that thanks to Jesus, I was content with being exactly as I was and I found this so liberating.

It was only once my love for Jesus was on the top spot of my heart and I truly found my delight in the Lord that I was ready and able to share my love with another because now it would be in the correct order. Jesus first and my husband second. I can love my husband better when I put Christ first because we actually make better spouses when God reigns within our hearts! We become more loving, more gracious, more merciful, more forgiving and less demanding. It's in the interest of both parties to have Jesus at the head of a marriage.

I think it's worthy to note here, the moulding and shaping never ends! When you get married a whole new level of moulding and shaping comes into play, it doesn't stop when you become a husband or wife! Hopefully we are always seeking to be moulded and shaped into the image of Christ whatever our walk in life may be. Single, married, engaged, it's about growing in the Lord and always remembering that Jesus is our First Love. I guess you could say that we're all "Still In Moulding!"

CASE DISMISSED

INSPIRATION

There are three main areas of inspiration for my poem "Case Dismissed." The first is a particular verse from the Bible which is 1 John 2:1 which reads,

"My dear children, I write this to you so that you will not sin. But if anybody does sin, we have one who speaks to the Father in our defence-Jesus Christ, the Righteous One."

The first time I read this verse the message really jumped out and hit me! The power of the words made such an impact on me that I stopped everything I was doing and thought about what I'd just read.

What this particular Scripture did was it really personalised my Saviour to me. It told me that not only does Jesus know my name and exactly who I am but He also takes the time to defend me in spite of all my flaws! This just amazed me! It filled me with a new level of adoration for Him and helped me understand a little more about how great His love is for me.

When I heard my Pastor give a teaching on this particular Scripture it really brought back all the initial feelings I'd had when I first read the passage. What it also did though was it gave me a much deeper knowledge and understanding of exactly what goes on in the realms of Heaven between Jesus and Satan. This equipped me to put my thoughts and feelings down on paper and these two areas of inspiration have very much influenced the second half of my poem.

The first half is inspired by something I heard the following week at my Church during Praise and Worship. The Praise and Worship leader was none other than my future husband Jan although of course I didn't know this at the time! He often sings his own songs during

Worship and on this particular day he played one that I hadn't heard before called "Seek The Truth." I heard him sing the lyrics "Only You could endure the Cross I nailed You to." I replayed those words in my mind and thought about what I'd just heard.

"Only You could endure the Cross I nailed you to!"

Now obviously as a born-again Christian I already knew that Jesus died on the Cross for me but what this particular wording did was it personalised the Crucifixion scene. I realised it had been too simple for me before to picture other people in that scene. I had imagined crowds taunting Him and men nailing Him to the Cross but now suddenly I was right in the centre of it! What I could see in my mind's eye now was me physically nailing Jesus to the Cross! Considering it was because of me and for me that He went through such horrendous torture I knew it might as well have been me driving the nails through His hands and feet.

What hit me the hardest however was the realisation that in spite of the pain and anguish I put Him through Jesus still loved me. So yet again I was driven to my knees in humility and was bowled over at the deeper knowledge of what my Saviour went through for me.

It was at that moment that I thought of how this complemented the feelings I'd had on the 1 John 2:1 passage the week before. For me to fully appreciate what it is that I have in Jesus as my defence I have to first understand what it is He's done for me by dying on the Cross. With these thoughts and feelings in place I decided to write "Case Dismissed."

POEM

I picture God the Father as He sits upon His throne.
I praise the Lord and sing His name, He does not sit alone.
For to His right, just by His side there sits the Righteous One;
My Lord and Saviour Jesus Christ. God's one and only Son.

I think of how He bore the Cross, forsaken on the Tree.
He hung with shame and paid the price and died thinking of me.
Though He was pure and lived a life completely free from sin,
The cup of wrath Christ took as His and did not pass from Him.

When soldiers came with grasping hands my Lord did not resist.
He did not flee or turn away when by a traitor kissed.
He knew the purpose of His life, the reason He had come;
To save the likes of you and me, a work that must be done.

When questioned by authorities my King did not proclaim
His innocence or righteousness, instead He took the blame.
So silently He stood condemned and shamed for all to see.
He took the guilt that *I* deserved and with humility.

I wonder, as they flogged His back what pain He felt within.
The whip that tore away His flesh was coated in *my* sin.
My lustful heart that ripped His beard, my lies spat in His face.
The vanity in me so vile instead was *His* disgrace.

My selfishness laid on His back He carried up the hill.
They kicked and mocked my mighty Lord and yet He loved me still.
My envy crowned upon His head, it pierced His gentle skin.
The injudicious crowd threw taunts as blood dripped down his chin.

As jealous whispers tied him down my Lord did not retreat.
My greed, the force that drove the nails into His hands and feet.
In tortured isolation and exposed for all to see,
My King endured shame on the Cross and died thinking of me!

His death was ignominious, it leaves no room to boast
For Christ became the essence of the thing He hated most!
The Father separated them, be under no pretence.
This torture burst the heart of Christ the pain was so intense.

Full willingly He hung with shame, a ransom paid for many.
There is no debt beside my name for Christ paid every penny.
My vindication bought through Him, set free from every wrong.
Forever more I'll serve my King, to Him I now belong.

But in the realms of Heaven there exists a battle fierce
For day and night with fiery darts there Satan tries to pierce
My righteous standing with the Lord and have it over thrown.
His fallacy is thinking that this standing is my own.

Venomous and vituperative he vilifies my name,
Listing my iniquities and highlighting my shame.
He cogently will state my flaws and criticise my life.
Insisting that the Lord should judge my every woe and strife.

"She has no right to come to You!" he'll hiss through putrid breath.
"If You're so "Holy" judge her now! The wages of sin is death!"
This vile, pernicious creature knows my every flaw to tell.
"The fiery pit's where she deserves eternity to dwell!"

I flee to Christ in penitence and fall down at the Cross.
I realise my sentence had He not suffered such loss.
Expedient was Jesus' work, His task though onerous,
Makes Satan's claims so fallible and so erroneous.

He stands in Heaven's courtroom and attempts hit after hit.
I will not fear for there is Christ, celestial advocate.
Destructive words from Satan's mouth reveal his fervent hate.
I know with Jesus there I stand complete and exculpate.

Absolved through Jesus, Christ my Lord, my Saviour, Heaven sent.
Authority so ultimate, His work preeminent.
Although God's Law declares my death, I know I've been set free!
Propitiation held in Christ, it's there for you and me.

The debt is paid, the work complete, there need not be another.
There is no cause beyond His reach, no sin His blood won't cover.
No longer do I stand condemned for there at Calvary,
Unlimited atonement bought imputed onto me.

So now there is no record of my sins beside my name.
They're blotted out forever for my Saviour took the blame.
This work the Devil cannot touch, he cannot take away
What Jesus Christ achieved for us on Crucifixion Day.

So when accused by Satan though I know my name is mud,
The covenant that Christ provides is written in His blood.
What happens then when Satan dares bring out my sinful list?
Christ lifts His palms, His scars on show, announcing
"Case Dismissed."

SCRIPTURE REFERENCES

Romans 8:1; 1 Corinthians 15:21-22; 2 Corinthians 5:17

AFTERWORD

I had a lady contact me through my website one evening asking if she could have permission to use this poem in a poetry recital competition that she was taking part in. I said she was very welcome to use it and wished her all the best. A few weeks later she got in touch again to let me know she had won the regional round and was now going on to compete in the International stage! I congratulated her and said I would be praying for her in this final round. I was over the moon to hear not too long afterwards that she had won the International competition too!

It blesses me beyond words to hear that the Lord is using the poetry and I always love to hear of the different ways they branch out. I'm not sure if the competition was a Christian event but one thing is certain, whoever was in the room that night heard the Gospel!

Stumpy-Footed Pigeon

Inspiration

It never ceases to amaze me how inspiration can appear from anywhere and at any time. My inspiration for "Stumpy-Footed Pigeon" was, as you may have already guessed, a stumpy-footed pigeon!

For anyone who has ever visited or lived in London you'll know how many scruffy, scraggly looking pigeons there are around! It was while I was waiting for a train one very cold day on the platform of Hammersmith Tube Station that one of these poor little feathered creatures got my mind ticking. The pigeon, looking rather worse for wear, hobbled past me on two stubby little legs with barely a toe in sight. My heart immediately went out to the sorry looking bird and I found myself thinking, "Poor stumpy-footed pigeon."

I went on to think about how hard life is for a pigeon living in busy London town and how the effects of their difficult little lives can often be seen in their dirty, misshapen appearance. I concluded however that as long as the pigeon had his wings he was equipped with what he needed to survive and this brought a small smile to my face regarding the pigeon's welfare! I certainly took great joy in watching him fly away.

I then thought about how hostile London is towards anyone living in the city and not just towards the pigeons! From some narrow corridor in my mind I recalled that in the book of Isaiah God is described as being our wings. The verse I was thinking of was Isaiah 40:31 which reads,

"But those who wait on the Lord shall renew their strength; they shall mount up with wings like eagles, they shall run and not be weary, they shall walk and not faint."

I then began to use my initial thoughts towards the stumpy-footed pigeon to draw observations and parallels from my own life and daily challenges as a resident of London. I thought about how these hardships and difficulties can take their toll and almost feel crippling at times.

Knowing that as long as I have Jesus Christ lifting me up and giving me strength to soar however, I too am fully equipped with all I need to survive, just like the stumpy-footed pigeon!

POEM

Oh stumpy-footed pigeon, you hobble down the street.
I watch you struggle round a bench on stumpy little feet.
Your steps are small and awkward as you search for scraps of food.
Your day-long task looks tiresome, I'd help you if I could.

Poor stumpy-footed pigeon, you're the only one who knows
Where you left your pigeon claws and little pigeon toes.
Perhaps on wired fencing that caught you like a vice
Or maybe in the dust and dirt beside the train track mice.

Oh stumpy-footed pigeon, your sorrow's clear to see.
To find a bird with all his toes is quite a rarity.
Your days are never easy, your pigeon life looks tough.
The busy streets of London town will always treat you rough.

I cannot help but ponder as I watch you in your strife,
The toll the city takes no matter who you are in life.
I start to notice passers by who go about their day.
It seems that London life comes with a hefty price to pay.

I see a stressed-out businessman who rushes with his case.
He bustles past and hurries off as if he'll win the race.
He elbows people left and right to gain that step ahead.
He could slow down and show some care but barges on instead.

I hear a crying baby as it's pushed along by Mum.
The giant buggy weighs her down, that doesn't look like fun.
She hauls the hefty carrier inside a busy train.
Commuters blankly stare at her, from helping they refrain.

This thoughtless, selfish mindset I just cannot understand.
They'd rather watch her struggle than to lend a helping hand!
It seems the city numbs the mind to focus on one's self.
To climb the ladder, gain the lead! It's each man for himself!

It's like a crazy rat race where it lacks a friendly tone.
Despite the crowds around me I feel terribly alone.
Anonymous, it's easy for a person to feel lost
For each pursues their own intent no matter of the cost.

I watch the weary masses as they trundle down the street.
I realise in London town we *all* have "stumpy feet!"
The daily pressures people face can really take their toll.
They beat you down and wear you out or worse, destroy your soul.

I start reflecting on myself, on troubles in *my* life.
The worries that can plague my mind and cut me like a knife.
The cost of living, friendships lost, what's next in my career?
This panic starts to build like an impending wave of fear.

Concerns can grow gargantuan, I feel I cannot cope.
I know I cannot take this stress and start to lose all hope.
I feel my soul is plummeting into the darkest night
But just as panic takes a hold I'm rescued by God's light.

He sends His Holy Comforter, He hears my desperate plea.
He reaches in and grabs my fear and takes it far from me.
Aware the hands around my throat have lost their grip of death,
I feel God's reassurance now with each and every breath.

Reminding me He's in control despite life's dreadful pains.
With reverence and submission I will gladly pass the reins.
For Jesus is the Rock on which my feet are firmly landing.
A quiet peace He gives me that transcends all understanding.

I dwell on words of Scripture and the praise Isaiah sings,
"I'll run and not grow weary," I have *Jesus* as my wings!
I focus on the promises I hadn't seen before;
He'll give me strength and raise me up, like eagles we can soar!

So now *within* my circumstance my heart is overjoyed.
I feel elation lift my soul although I'm unemployed!
Though changing aspects of my life can make me feel unsure,
I know *unchanging love* in Christ. With Jesus I'm secure.

This knowledge makes me slow things down, take each day at a time.
Just set my sights on Jesus Christ, I know I will be fine!
I know at times frustration has me pulling at my hair
But worry's not a burden Christ intended me to bear.

The fear of the unknown can cause my mind to fuss and buzz.
I don't know where I'm going but I know the One who does.
I re-think my priorities and once this is addressed,
I look at all He's given me and realise I'm blessed.

No matter how life cripples me and pins me to the ground,
I know with Jesus as my wings there's freedom to be found.
So stumpy-footed pigeon, not so different now from me,
I smile and watch you spread your wings and fly away so free.

Scripture References

Matthew 6:25-34

MUD IN MY EYES

INSPIRATION

This poem was written when I was going through a season full of change, uncertainty and persecution. One morning during this time I was doing some Bible study and I was taken to the passage of John 9:1-11 which reads,

"As he went along, he saw a man blind from birth. His disciples asked him, "Rabbi, who sinned, this man or his parents, that he was born blind?"

"Neither this man nor his parents sinned," said Jesus, "but this happened so that the works of God might be displayed in him. As long as it is day, we must do the works of him who sent me. Night is coming, when no one can work. While I am in the world, I am the light of the world."

After saying this, he spit on the ground, made some mud with the saliva, and put it on the man's eyes. "Go," he told him, "wash in the Pool of Siloam." So the man went and washed, and came home seeing.

His neighbours and those who had formerly seen him begging asked, "Isn't this the same man who used to sit and beg?" Some claimed that he was.

Others said, "No, he only looks like him."

But he himself insisted, "I am the man."

"How then were your eyes opened?" they asked.

He replied, "The man they call Jesus made some mud and put it on my eyes. He told me to go to Siloam and wash. So I went and washed, and then I could see."

After reading this passage I felt inspired to write a poem entitled "Mud In My Eyes."

POEM

Whenever I read of my Saviour I feel my heart lift, how it sings.
He displayed perfect love for His people and did truly
miraculous things.
He restored crippled limbs in an instant, drove out demons by raising
His hand.
He could heal every illness or defect, even storms would obey
His command.

Some were healed just by touching His clothing, He fed thousands with
fish and some bread.
He could walk on tempestuous water, brought a young girl back from
the dead.
He is truly a wonderful Saviour, one like Him I never will find.
He came to give life to His people, He came to give sight to the blind.

When I read of the man at Siloam and the process of how he
was cured
I can feel how my heart is encouraged and my spirit and soul reassured.
Though Jesus could heal in a moment, He put the man's faith to
the test.
He had to obey His commandment and believe in His words to
be blessed.

I ponder the feelings he went through, was he fearful Christ's words
could be lies?
Did he doubt in the goodness of Jesus as he walked there with mud in
his eyes?
Hesitation and doubt he discarded and decided on Christ he
would lean.
He believed every word from His Saviour, from a Man he had not
even seen!

What a truly magnificent witness, strongest faith that no doubt
could defeat.
I aspire to live with such boldness, this obedience I wish to repeat.
I will lay at God's feet in submission, with His help any trial I'll
get through.
If a man blind from birth can believe Him then I can believe in
Christ too.

Though others may think that I'm foolish and fear that they'll see
my demise
I know I'm obeying my Saviour and I'm walking with mud in my eyes.
Although I can't see where I'm going, I *do* know this pathway is right.
He's testing my faith and obedience, in *His* time He'll give me my sight.

I have to be trusting in Jesus, believe and obey His commands.
The worries that life heaps upon me I'll pass into God's mighty hands.
He *could* reveal all in an instant and save me from shedding a tear
But He's moulding and teaching me daily to trust in Him
and persevere.

Long suffering is what I must go through if I want to be close to
my King.
Through these trials I'll learn of His goodness and the joy that His
comfort can bring.
In these difficult times He is with me, of this fact I can always be sure
And I'll never go through any hardship that my Saviour did not
first endure.

He isn't a God who is distant, He hears all my pitiful cries.
Understanding, He feels all my heart ache. With my anguish He
can empathise.
With this knowledge I feel Him much closer, I know I'm not
walking alone.
I'm trusting in Jesus to guide me, my Father still sits on His Throne.

For He is the One who is sovereign and leads through all aspects of life.
He's there when my heart is rejoicing and there when I'm stricken
through strife.
He's promised that He'll never leave me and the weight of my
burdens relieve.
He created the Earth and the Heavens! In Jesus I choose to believe!

My life is not governed by treasures or abundance of things I possess.
I will look to my Lord for the answers for my pain I don't have
to suppress.
His love is not measured by money or success in my chosen career.
If I know in His eyes I'm accepted then it leaves me with nothing
to fear.

How foolish to doubt in His goodness, He will keep me from
wandering far.
Through my faith I can witness to others, with His help I can shine like
a star.
So wide and so deep is God's loving, what can separate me from
this love?
No trial or deep tribulation for He's caring for me from above.

If I may be so bold as to ask you what you're putting *your* trust in today,
If it's anything other than Jesus then know it will all blow away.
Can the walls of your house withstand fire, your possessions stay safe
from a thief?
If you trust that your money will save you then this is a foolish belief.

You can't buy your way into Heaven or enter the Gates by good works.
With humility, trust in our Saviour but immune we are not to
life's hurts.
Though He asks me to walk through this valley, I am blind and know
not where it leads
But according to riches in Jesus my Father will meet all my needs!

To the secular eye it is folly, my submission seems foolish and weak
But I know His Kingdom and righteousness come first and are what I
must seek.
God's purpose for me is a good one though it may seem I've taken
a fall.
My vision is blurred and impaired now but I'm walking with Him who
sees all.

He's building me up to lack nothing, all these trials I must conquer
and face.
Every day I'll submit to His purpose and get through it by God's
saving grace.
I mustn't just think of the temporal for this hardship I cannot compare
To the joy that awaits me in Heaven! So my cross I will take up
and bear.

Though this battle may seem never ending, make me feel that I want to
give in,
If it means I'm drawn closer to Jesus then I'll walk every mile next
to Him.
I know in the end I'll see clearly, I'll look back at this time with surprise
For I'll see where this journey has led me though I walked it with mud
in my eyes.

SCRIPTURE REFERENCES

2 Corinthians 5:7; Proverbs 3:5-6; Psalm 119:105

SAVE SOME

"Save Some" is a poem about sharing the Gospel and one of my main sources of inspiration was a quote by the 19th Century Preacher Charles Spurgeon. He said,

"Save some O Christians! By all means save some! From yonder flames and outer darkness. And from the weeping, wailing and gnashing of teeth, seek to save some. Let this, as in the case of the apostle be your great, ruling object in life, that by all means you might save some!"

This quote really made me think about the consequences of not knowing or rejecting Jesus Christ and the reality of judgment day. It filled me with an urgency to share the truth and the good news of redemption through Jesus while there is still time.

A few months before I read this particular quote I had heard a sermon where the speaker used an analogy to describe the position a Christian is in when it comes to the importance of sharing the Gospel. The analogy compared this world to a house in perilous danger, perhaps with a gas leak or already on fire with the Christian being aware of the coming danger. He went on to say that we have the responsibility to alert the other "inhabitants," thus giving them the chance to escape too.

The speaker talked about the privilege of knowing the Gospel and how we must try to share this with people we come into contact with no matter what the outcome may be. He explained that although the Christian can't control how the person reacts to the Gospel, it is the responsibility of the Christian to share the Gospel in love. He went on to encourage us as believers to give people the information they need to know to make an informed decision about their future.

I felt that this emphasised the feelings stirred up within me by Spurgeon's quote and I decided to turn the analogy into a dream sequence. I soon began to write a poem about sharing the wonderful, soul-saving Gospel of Jesus Christ.

POEM

Last night as I rested in slumber a curious thing happened to me;
I dreamt that I slept in a mansion with my friends and my dear family.
Now our settings were rather dramatic, a mansion house deep in
the wood.
The vast, velvet sky lay above us creating a dark, somber mood.

I dreamt that I woke from my slumber and was making my way down
the hall
When a pungent and deadly scent hit me. I knew trouble this house
would befall.
I dreamt of a terrible poison that would kill every soul in it's path.
Insidious it hissed through the hallway, intent to devour with wrath.

I could dash down the stairs in an instant, through the door and to
safety I'd run
But my heart felt a burden to rescue, to remain and to try to save some!
I raced back to warn all the others, to alert them and try to get through.
I was driven by sheer desperation. I must reach them, of this fact
I knew.

Now whether they chose to believe me, it wasn't for me to decide.
My job was to warn them in earnest and to know in my heart I
had tried.
How on Earth could I leave them to perish when I knew of the danger
to come?
With all effort I'd try to awaken, with a passion I'd try to save some!

I entered the first room I came to and rushed to the body asleep,
I threw back the covers in panic 'til they fell on the floor in a heap.
I desperately shook them in earnest feeling hope as they opened
their eyes.
"What's the matter?" they said in confusion, staring straight at my face
in surprise.

"Dearest one please awake and just listen. Pay attention to all I will say.
I must warn you, such danger is coming! Take heed and escape
right away!"
Though I emphasised time was of essence and encouraged them now to
make haste.
They dawdled and gathered belongings, precious time that they thought
they could waste.

"Run *now* while you can!" I would tell them but I'd watch as they'd
procrastinate.
I feared that they'd find more excuses and feared that they'd leave it
too late.
"Please listen dear friend as I tell you of the terrible danger to come!"
But they left me no choice but to leave them, to continue and try to
save some!

So I dashed through the hall seeking others, the air was like foul,
fetid breath.
My skin crawled at the presence of evil, I recoiled at the nearness
of death
But this filled me with new resolution to push onward and
never retreat.
My plight was more urgent than ever for this evil I couldn't defeat.

Door after door I would run to, some responded and heeded my call
But I soon realised on this journey that I wouldn't get through to
them all.
"You must open your eyes!" I would beg them. "Do not let my words
fall on deaf ears!
For the evil that quickly approaches, it's much worse than your darkest
of fears!"

I was filled with a deep desperation for no matter how hard I would try
They'd declare that this "danger" was folly and to them it just did
not apply.
They would turn me away in their anger and accept not the trouble
they'd reap.
They refused to take heed to my warnings and instead chose the
darkness of sleep.

So in sorrow and anguish I left them for my worries I'd tried hard
to voice
But resistant they stayed to the signals, making clear that they'd now
made their choice.
Their stubbornness blinded their judgment and their hearts were now
hardened and tough
Yet for others not one word was needed for my *actions* were
warning enough.

They responded, alerted to danger and together we ran down the hall.
We were fleeing the ominous warnings and we chose to embrace
freedom's call.
With our hearts beating faster than ever, closer still to the door we
were drawn.
It was then that we noticed the glimmers of the crystal clear light of
the dawn.

As we spilled through the door to our freedom liberated by heeding
the truth,
We knew we'd escaped darkest anguish and would live ever more in
our youth.
As we turned to look back for the others and I pictured their faces
and names,
I was ravaged by sadness and horror as I watched the house go up
in flames.

For the evil had taken it's victims though salvation was offered for free
But their ears wouldn't open to listen and their eyes wouldn't open
to see.
Such joy that I felt for the rescued, utter sorrow I felt for the lost.
This ambivalence tore at my spirit. "I must save some whatever
the cost!"

With these words on my lips I shot upright and I sat on my bed
wide awake.
Then I pictured each face of a loved one and again I could feel my
heart break
For the lies of the devil are tempting, they are cleverly subtle you see.
They convince countless souls in believing they have no cause to worry,
they're free.

But these spurious words are repulsive for they're dripping with lies
and deceit.
Our salvation rests solely with Jesus and for those who will fall at
His feet.
He provides an escape for His loved ones, vindicates the
eternally damned.
We gain life and sanctification and attain it by taking His hand.

The freedom I've found with my Saviour! The Light of the world
I've seen!
Salvation that beckons and glimmers just like the door in my dream
For Christ is the passage to safety, to escape we must all run to Him.
If we're not liberated through Jesus then we're slaves and still dead in
our sin.

For Satan has mastered deception and his lies, often small and unseen,
They will claim every soul they encounter, like the poisonous gas in
my dream.
But there *is* an escape that's on offer if we look to Christ's beautiful face.
Undeserving, I choose to accept Him and His gift I will gladly embrace.

I now have redemption in Jesus, my salvation the devil can't touch.
I walk through the glittering doorway Christ provided, He loves us
so much.
This joy I must share with my loved ones for the door isn't there for
just me.
I desire they wake up and listen and I pray that they all be set free!

Such joy that I feel for the rescued, utter sorrow I feel for the lost.
This ambivalence tears at my spirit, I must save some whatever the cost!
I must warn them with fervent conviction for *I know* of the judgment
to come.
How then can I call myself Christian if I don't try my best to save some?

Now I know it's not *me* who can save them but my efforts I
mustn't restrict.
My call is to stay true and faithful and then let the *Spirit* convict.
For He is the One who will guide them, the One who can truly suffice
In leading each soul to their Saviour, their redemption found only
in Christ.

So whether they choose to believe me, it isn't for me to decide.
My job is to warn them in earnest and to know in my heart I
have tried.
So I ask you dear brethren to join me for we know not when judgment
will come.
Until then we must try to awaken. Until then we must try to save some!

SCRIPTURE REFERENCES

2 Corinthians 2:15-17; 1 Corinthians 9:22-23; Romans 5:9

THE GIRL WITHIN THE PICTURE

INSPIRATION

In order to explain how I came to write this poem I feel it's important to share my testimony first. It gives a backdrop and "sets the stage" for my inspiration you might say!

I was very blessed in the sense that when I was growing up my Mum took me and my sister each week to Church and brought the Word of God into our lives at an early age. We went to a Church called Calvary Christian Fellowship in Motherwell which is Pastored by David Simpson.

I know that as a young girl I had a relationship with Jesus and I always knew that He was real. His presence within my heart was very clear to me and even in my childlike understanding of things He spoke directly into my life and made His existence known to me.

I remember that each night before I went to sleep I'd be lying in bed and I would pray to Him. I would just talk to the Lord about all the kinds of things that might concern a small a child. Of course when I look back now at the prayers I can see how trivial these things were in the grand scale of life but they weren't trivial to me at the time and therefore they weren't trivial to Jesus. He would give me a peace in my heart about whatever it was I was concerned about. I knew that as His daughter my prayers were listened to. My loving Heavenly Father always helped me in my situations and showed me that He cared about the details of my life.

Sadly, despite the closeness that I enjoyed with God as a child, my attitude started to change as I got into my early teens. I began to wander away from Him in my thoughts and I felt like I wanted to live life my way and that I knew better than God about what was right and what was good for me. Imagine thinking you can know better than the One who created you!

By the time I was eighteen I was ready to head off to college to train in Musical Theatre. This of course wasn't a bad thing to pursue, Musical Theatre is hardly the worst thing you can do with your life and I was using the skills God had given me. What was wrong with this situation however was that the pursuit of my career was now the biggest thing in my life and the issue was that I loved it more than I loved God.

You could say that my desire to perform had become my idol. As I try to explain to young adults if I'm ever sharing Jesus with them, idols don't need to be statues of Buddha or pillars of gold or something. An idol is just whatever we place in importance above God. It may take on the form of a boyfriend or girlfriend, an iPhone, a TV program, an obsession with our appearance or physique or time spent training at the gym. Whatever we give priority to in our lives and whatever sits on the top seat in our hearts, if it isn't Jesus Christ then it's an idol. It might be a good thing in and of itself but if we put it before Jesus then it's become something that we idolise and therefore is our idol. My chosen career path had certainly become mine.

It was what I dedicated most of my energy to and it was very much my greatest desire in life. The idea of involving God in my plans and asking Him for guidance sadly was pretty far from my thoughts and if I did pray it wasn't to genuinely seek God's will for me. Instead of seeking His wisdom in my life I'd just ask Him to bless me in my plans which of course isn't a proper prayer. I wasn't thinking about using my life to serve God and go where He guided me for His glory, it was all about me. It was all about doing what I wanted to do, going where I wanted to go and for my glory!

When I think back to this time what I can see most clearly is God's grace. Even though I wasn't really acknowledging Him at this point He never took His eyes away from me. I think He just gave me a long rope to go out into the world and discover for myself how empty it is without Him.

In terms of my career, if you had asked me when I was training what show I would most like to be in I'd have definitely said "Fame." When I was offered a role in this show at the age of twenty three you can imagine how excited I was! I was over the moon because this was what I had been training for all these years! I felt that I had finally "arrived" if you like and this would be the thing that would make me happier than I had ever been.

It's interesting to note that during my time in this show I was completely miserable. It wasn't that I didn't enjoy being in the show, it's just that performing in the West End didn't fulfil me in the way that I had thought it would. It certainly didn't live up to my expectations.

Looking back I know that my heartache and brokenness was down to the fact that I was lonely because I had turned my back on God. Yes I was using the gifts He gave me but it wasn't combined with His fellowship so I missed my Saviour. I had known the joy of His companionship in my life and I had left my first love and tried to replace Him with another. I discovered that Jesus cannot be replaced. There's a place in our hearts that belongs only to Him and He showed me that nothing else in this world can fit there.

What I find really interesting is when I hear other people's testimonies or read about certain people in the Bible and they have everything stripped away from them. When this happens it often seems to leave the person able to see their acute need and desire for God but I feel like this is the opposite of how God worked in me.

I feel like Jesus looked into my heart, saw what I was striving for and placing before Him in importance then in His gentle, loving and gracious way He gave me the very things I was idolising. He let me discover for myself the emptiness and the futility of what this world has to offer if it isn't combined with the joy and peace of knowing you're in the centre of God's will. It doesn't matter how good the "gig" is, if it isn't alongside Jesus it's a miserable and empty place to be.

In hindsight I can see how the Lord used this time to speak to my spirit and get me to the place I needed to be where I prayed a proper prayer and I called out to Him in repentance. I wanted Him and I now found myself desiring His closeness and His fellowship again above all else. My Father welcomed me back with open arms and showed me what wonderful forgiveness there is to be found in Jesus!

Having explained the lead up to writing this poem I can now go on to say that my inspiration came during one ordinary day in 2008 when

I was doing the housework of all things! I picked up a picture frame to dust it and for some reason I decided to spend a few seconds looking at the picture within the frame. I found myself smiling as I looked at an image of myself sitting with a friend of mine.

The photograph was taken when two friends and I were on a holiday in 2006 and it was during this time that I was still trying to ignore God and deny my need and desire for Him in my life. It became apparent to me that the smile on my face was nothing more than a mask. It was a lie to cover up the true pain and sorrow going on inside and all of a sudden I could see right through it.

As I stood there looking at the picture I began to feel a whole host of negative feelings towards myself for not using that time to serve God. Right in that very instant however I felt the gentleness of the Holy Spirit draw alongside me and encourage me not to feel hatred towards myself because God didn't.

Again I was blown away by my awesome Saviour. Even in the process of writing this poem I feel that Jesus revealed more of His caring and loving nature to me. I'm eternally grateful to my wonderful God for showing such incredible patience, mercy and forgiveness towards the girl within the picture.

POEM

With absent thoughts and gentle song I dusted on the shelf.
I noticed then in front of me a picture of myself.
Without much care I picked it up and looked deep in my eyes,
Remembering the girl I was I came to realise
Although the smile upon my face implied no hint of grief,
I still re-called the broken heart that lay just underneath.

For in that time I knew You not and lived in shadows dark,
Reflections of a weary soul where life had left it's mark.
An empty shell so meaningless, no purpose, point or truth.
My life adrift so aimlessly, a waste of precious youth.
I tried to find the answers but knew none of them were true.
I wouldn't find the peace I sought until I looked for You.

Though outwardly I had success my heart could feel no pride.
I knew my life was meaningless, my soul was dead inside.
The worldly joys so temporal would leave me wanting more,
They left me with an empty void much bigger than before.
The hollow offers of the world could never satiate,
I knew the very things I'd sought I'd soon begin to hate.

They couldn't fill the longing that I felt now deep within.
I knew I needed You Lord and to let go of my sin.
You used this time to waken me and see my need for You.
You reached into my circumstance and let Your light shine through.
Forever grateful I will be, Your love you did bestow.
You never took Your eyes from me, You wouldn't let me go.

So as I stood, I thought of all the shame I put You through.
The pain You must have suffered in my years apart from You.
You watched as I ignored Your Word and went off on my way.
I added to the pain You felt on Crucifixion day.
This thought aroused such wrenching guilt, dark feelings drawing near
But just before they took control You whispered in my ear.

"Don't punish and chastise yourself for what you were before.
Remember, it's just you before you chose the narrow door.
The girl who fights so hard for Me and stands up for My name,
Well she's the one you stare at now and look upon with shame.
You look at her with deep contempt, resentment and disgust
But listen child, that girl is *you*. The one in whom I trust."

"I saw beyond your sinful ways and reached into your heart.
I gave you life and hope anew, I gave you a fresh start.
Your guilt and shame can haunt you but whenever this begins,
Remember that I died for you when *still* dead in your sins.
Don't dwell on your iniquities or see mistakes you made
For love and justice kiss the Cross and now your debt is paid."

"Although you were a slave to sin and spiritually blind,
My precious daughter, worry not and leave your past behind.
I choose to not remember your transgressions or your shame.
I only feel My love for you, now you should do the same.
You're now a new creation and in Christ your sin can hide.
The time you spent enslaved to sin has washed away and died."

"Desires of your carnal mind will now have passed away.
Contentment I can promise as you walk with Me each day.
Rejoice in your new nature and embrace divine exchange
For now our friendship is secure and this will *never* change.
You face no condemnation for My promises are true,
You've purity in Christ and now My Spirit dwells in you."

"I came to give you life, that you may live abundantly.
Your life is counter cultural but in harmony with Me.
Although you'll battle with the flesh, when tempted, don't give in
For now you're filled with power and can overcome your sin.
Stand firm and set your sights on Me, I'll see you through it all.
Adorn My armour, use your gifts and heed my every call."

"Do not be swayed by disbelief or thrown by foolish talk
For Satan envies what we have so stay true in your walk.
He'll try hard to convince you that you're "governed" by My "rules"
But know you're walking in the truth so heed no word from fools.
The boundaries I set will keep you safe from the corrupt.
A life without parameters will only self-destruct."

"You know the anguish you endured without My loving touch.
I could not leave you in your sin, I love you far too much.
For you are My creation child, in you I am displayed
And in My sight you're fearfully and *wonderfully* made.
My love for you runs faster than the rivers and the lakes.
Remember that I chose you and I do not make mistakes."

With new found peace I placed the picture back upon the shelf,
So grateful that this face did not reflect my current self.
I'd contemplate the lengths and darkest depths to which You'd go
To blot out my iniquities and make me white as snow.
I realised without You Lord, within me there's no good.
I then resolved anew to live in humble servitude.

The girl within the picture, she's so far and yet so near.
I view her with compassion now I know You loved her dear.
I worship You, O Sovereign Lord, Your love has set me free!
You took my life and gave me hope and saw the worth in me.
Your heart is filled with mercy Lord, despite my every flaw,
You saved me from my sin and now I bow to You in awe.

SCRIPTURE REFERENCES

1 Corinthians 1:26-31

AFTERWORD

Thankfully God is faithful even when we are not but I could have saved myself a lot of heartache if I had just stayed true to Jesus from the start. I think if my testimony has a moral in any way it would be "Choose Jesus!" Save yourself a lot of heartache and lot of wasted time and choose Jesus!

If you've already chosen Him as your Saviour, hallelujah! Hosts of Heaven have rejoiced over you! Now if I may, I'd like to encourage you to continue to put Jesus first and choose Him daily. Choose Him as your Friend, choose Him as your Guide, your Leader and your Confidante. Choose Him above and before anything or anyone else in life. You and the people around you will benefit for it.

If you haven't chosen Him already, what are you waiting for? What is it in your life that you love more than Him? I promise you it's not worth trading in your salvation for. Let it go. Give it to Jesus and He will take care of you. I'd really like to encourage you today to accept Him as your Saviour. Jesus loves you and He wants you, the question is, do you want Him? He is your Creator, He came to Earth for you, paid for your sins on the Cross and rose again. He's the one, true, living God and He longs for you to get to know Him personally.

The devil tried to convince me not to commit my life to Jesus with all sorts of bribe attempts. I feared I would lose all my friends, miss out on great work opportunities and become someone people didn't respect or want to know. Jesus' influence in my heart overruled this however and He won the battle for my soul, praise the Lord! I am so grateful that God is patient and that He pursued me. He mercifully chose me and I gladly chose Him in August of 2006. It was the best decision I ever made and I will never regret it.

EYES ON YOU

INSPIRATION

I'm sure many people can relate to me when I say there are seasons in life when you feel like you're going through trial after trial after trial. I've heard my Pastor say that as a Christian we're generally either going through a trial, coming out of one or just about to go into one! Not the most encouraging thought but probably very accurate! I often find myself thinking, "Thank goodness I have Jesus to help me!"

There are of course wonderful times of peace and rest but I was learning that it's when you're going through fiery trials that it's more important than ever to fix your eyes on Jesus. As a young, single woman living in London at the time of writing this poem I was incredibly grateful to find that I could rely on God to be my comfort and my strength in all situations. He really taught me a lot about turning to Him with my troubles and watching Him work through my circumstances.

Jesus also really showed me through this time that He will always provide what I need just as He promises in His Word and I discovered a close fellowship with my Saviour that I hadn't known before. I experienced first hand that unlike "happiness" which can be so fickle and fleeting, the joy of the Lord doesn't evaporate when things get tough. On the contrary. It's when situations are difficult that we can feel the joy and peace Christ brings to our hearts all the more, we just have to keep our eyes on Him!

POEM

Oh Father help me look to You, don't let me go astray.
Don't let me look at worldly things and go my worldly way.
I dared to think the storm had stilled, the waves had washed ashore
But now I feel the endless trials come crashing back for more.

They buffet me from every side, they bruise and burden me.
They beat me to a bloody pulp and pound relentlessly.
I re-gain my composure just to feel another blow
As fiery darts come sailing in from Satan's fiery bow.

Oh Father I am terrified, I thought I'd passed the test.
I thought I'd steered through waters rough and found a place of rest
But now the troubles carry on, the night descends anew.
Dear Abba, help me once again to fix my eyes on You.

I do not understand why I must ride this wave again,
I only know to look to You, my Saviour and my Friend.
I cling to You with desperate grip and hang tenaciously.
I beg of You O' Sovereign Lord to fare this storm with me.

I cannot seem to gain control, I tumble round and round.
I wonder when the tide will change and bring me solid ground.
I feel my strength depart as yet again I take a knock
But then resolve to look to You, my Lighthouse on the rock.

You silence noise inside my mind, You still my troubled heart.
Without You in the centre my whole life would fall apart.
You keep me held together like the strongest super-glue,
Please wash away my every fear and keep my eyes on You!

You soothe my sorrow like a balm and rinse away my pain.
Though salty tears may streak my face I smile and say Your name.
Your comfort is beyond compare, beyond all worldly things.
I do not serve a man-made god, I serve the King of kings!

Your thoughts of me out-number every tiny grain of sand.
My finite mind can fathom not nor ever understand
How much You deeply care for me and know what's good and right
For I am numbered with the saints, in whom is Your delight!

Whenever I am filled with doubt or start to loose my nerve
It's good that I re-call exactly *who* it is I serve!
Considering Your Heavens and the stars which You ordained,
What is man that each of us by You are loved and named?

Create in me the purest heart and purge my sins I pray.
Please lead me down Your path O Lord, the Everlasting Way.
So like the smoothest pebble lying on the salty shore,
The waves of tribulation make me smoother than before.

You take Your holy microscope, examining each part,
Refining every jagged edge and corner of my heart.
Exposing every darkened place I didn't know was there,
My hidden ways are drenched in light and all because You care.

I know these tests are not to punish or discourage me
But only when the water's hot can I then truly see
What wicked ways are lurking in this fallen heart of mine.
So in the midst of sorrow I cry "Not *my* will but Thine!"

Your ways are so efficient, every sin is sliced and diced.
You purge and purify my soul and make me more like Christ
For even though You slay me Lord, I still will hope in You.
Your mercies mean I'm not consumed, Your promises are true.

It's good that I should seek You, Your compassions never fail
And with Your strength I know I can embrace this and prevail.
Though weeping may consume the night, the devil can't destroy
The peace I have in knowing that the morning brings new joy.

My ever faithful, loving God, Thy Word does light my path.
I meditate and feel Your peace within this aftermath.
Your Godly eyes are fixed on me, You always see me through.
How wonderful I feel now that I've fixed *my* eyes on *You*!

My heart is now surrendered and submitted to Your will,
Sovereignty belongs to You and brings us closer still.
I realise with thoughts of You, I re-gain my aplomb.
As joy comes flooding from my heart my peace comes sailing home.

SCRIPTURE REFERENCES

Lamentations 3:22-26

PRECIOUS LITTLE BUNDLE

INSPIRATION

I've been blessed with two beautiful nephews and two wonderful nieces in my life and since the birth of the first ones in 2008 I've been discovering the joy that children can bring into a family. I wrote this poem especially for my oldest nephew when he was still a baby and read it at his dedication. My inspiration came from a heart of gratitude to God for blessing the family with such a wonderful gift. My nephew is certainly much bigger now but I still love to smother him in kisses and I'll always remember the days when he was just a precious little bundle!

POEM

Oh precious little bundle, oh treasured baby boy
You've captivated every heart and filled our lives with joy.
A gift from Christ our Saviour, our gentle Lord above
Delivered you into our keep to cherish and to love.

Born within the thoughts of Christ and made with Godly skill,
His mighty hands prepared you for His good and perfect will.
For you were knit together by the hands that formed the Earth!
He looked on us with favour and He blessed us with your birth.

Mirroring His image as He formed a new creation,
We catch a glimpse within your eyes of God's imagination!
Determining your character while sitting on His Throne,
His fingers formed your body in the secret place unknown.

Surrounding Him, the watchful eyes of Cherubim arose,
Admiring the craftsmanship of perfect baby toes!
The Author of all life at work! Behold, a sight to see!
We praise the Lord and bless the day that your life came to be.

For now He's placed you in our care to raise you in His ways
And teach you how to look to Him and trust Him all your days.
Appointing us with stewardship to guide you in your youth,
Endow you with the love of Christ and point you to the truth.

As we commit your life to God, protect him Lord we pray.
We dedicate this child to You and ask You bless the day.
This little one belongs to You, You've mapped out his life's plan.
Please mould his heart and help him grow into a godly man.

We ask for wisdom dearest Lord, for we must teach and guide.
We pray that in Your grace and truth he always will abide.
That he would seek to know You more with every passing year
And walk according to Your Word with reverence and with fear.

Please guide his steps and lead him through the times of woe and strife.
We pray he'll choose the King of kings, the One who *gave* him life!
Our dreams and aspirations for him grow with each day new,
Whatever he desires Lord, may he *delight* in You.

Please fill him with Your Spirit, with Your presence soft and meek.
May mighty things be done through Your creation so unique.
Father give him knowledge, make him spiritually astute,
A heart filled with compassion and a life that bears much fruit.

Although to us this little one may be a new addition,
You knew his name before You even laid the Earth's foundation!
Though we dream dreams, have wondrous thoughts and plans for him
to do,
No one has a *greater* plan than one ordained by You.

So as we give him back to You, we glorify Your name.
You've blessed our hearts and now our lives will never be the same.
Oh precious little bundle, oh treasured baby boy.
May love for Jesus guide your heart and fill your life with joy!

SCRIPTURE REFERENCES

Proverbs 22:6

AFTERWORD

This poem has been used a few times for friends' baby dedications over the years and my prayer is that it can continue to be used by anyone who feels it would be a blessing on their special day!

UNCLEAN

INSPIRATION

This poem was inspired by Mark 1:40-45 which reads,

"Now a leper came to Him, imploring Him, kneeling down to Him and saying to Him,
"If you are willing, You can make me clean."
Then Jesus, moved with compassion, stretched out His hand and touched him, and said to him,
"I am willing; be cleansed."
As soon as He had spoken, immediately the leprosy left him, and he was cleansed. And He strictly warned him and sent him away at once, and said to him,
"See that you say nothing to anyone; but go your way, show yourself to the priest, and offer for your cleansing those things which Moses commanded, as a testimony to them."
However, he went out and began to proclaim it freely, and to spread the matter, so that Jesus could no longer openly enter the city, but was outside in deserted places; and they came to Him from every direction."

When I first read this story of how Jesus heals the leper I was blown away by the compassion, love and grace He shows. The demonstration created an incredible picture in my mind's eye. I could clearly imagine the noisy, bustling crowds surrounding Him and competing for His attention along with the arrival of a man who would have been viewed as repulsive and unclean.

The leper would have broken the ceremonial law just to enter the house to see Jesus and then in turn Jesus broke the Levitical law by touching the leper in order to cleanse him. Rather than chastening him,

Jesus allowed His love for the man to overrule the law and seeing his faith, rewarded him openly by making him clean. This really spoke to my heart on how much Jesus loves His children and how He is faithful to forgive those who truly ask for forgiveness.

There have been times when I've felt embarrassed to be asking my Heavenly Father to forgive me for my sins and wondered if He ever finds me repulsive because of my failures. These verses revealing His love and grace really showed me how Jesus feels on this subject. They also showed me that our need for the grace of God is timeless and that no matter what we've done, where we've been or what condition we're in, if our hearts are truly repentant then we can always find mercy and forgiveness at the feet of our Saviour Jesus Christ.

POEM

I close my eyes and picture crowds of people all around.
I almost hear their dusty feet trampling the ground,
Competing for attention as they push and reach for Him.
He teaches with authority as thirsty souls flood in.

Within my mind, I stand as I observe this noisy scene
Then from the crowd a stricken voice declares itself "Unclean!"
With gasps and cries of horror, utter panic fills the room.
A dark, foreboding atmosphere then permeates the gloom.

Where just before the bustling crowds had pushed and fought to be,
The particles of clouds and dust are now all I can see.
The silence is unnerving as it hangs in stagnant air.
I feel the disapproval in the weight of every stare.

With bodies pinned against the walls, each covering their face,
Attention bores toward one man, a figure in disgrace.
His withered form is wrapped in cloth, his rags are far from fresh.
Offending every stomach, sickly smells of rotting flesh.

I find myself now sharing in their judgement and disgust.
Self righteousness unites us in resentment and distrust.
We stare at him together now with eyes that disapprove
And then I slowly realise that one Man didn't move.

When madness overtook each soul, consuming every heart,
When mayhem had engulfed the room I saw He took no part.
Instead with silent stillness He stood steadfast in His place
And now just yards between them, their eyes meeting face to face.

The tension almost palpable for what will happen now?
Improper interaction regulations won't allow!
The leper should not *dare* approach the One of high esteem!
Surely Jesus will announce, "Depart from me! Unclean!"

What happened next however violated every law.
The shock was punctuated with the dropping of each jaw
For right before our very eyes the leper lunged toward
The gentle One referred to as "Good Teacher," "Rabbi," "Lord."

Imploring Him so desperately and falling on his knees,
"If You are willing dearest Lord, You can cleanse me, please!"
The leper trembled at His feet, his very soul laid bare.
His supplication lined with God for Jesus heard his prayer.

Compassion filled this Saviour's heart and much to our surprise,
He gently touched this putrid form right before our eyes!
The leper's peeling, pallid skin was deemed untouchable
But Jesus saw that deep within repentance filled his soul.

Both men had broken through the law to set the leper free.
In disbelief we stared, such love displayed for all to see!
For none before had shown such selfless, sacrificial love.
This Man was different, set apart and sent from God above.

I feel my thoughts retreating now back to reality
And find my soul's been stirred within from what this verse shows me.
Although my fallen nature means I'm sinful through and through,
As long as I'm repentant Christ will *always* cleanse me too!

To think of how each day I find myself down on my knees
While asking for forgiveness for my flaws through desperate pleas.
It almost feels like blasphemy to ask of One so pure
To touch my sinful body but Christ's shown me He's the cure.

Although I don't have leprosy destroying healthy skin,
I *do* have faults and sinful ways that sully me within.
So like the leper I must seek forgiveness on my knees,
"Because You're willing gracious God, I ask You cleanse me please."

"According to Your tender mercies, purify I pray.
According to Your lovingkindness, wash me thoroughly.
Purge, refresh and cleanse me, from my sin please hide Your face.
Create in me a cleaner heart, O Giver of all grace."

"My tongue shall sing Your righteousness, my mouth bring forth Your praise.
Your mercy and compassion see me safely through my days.
A broken and a contrite heart You never will despise.
A spirit humbled at Your feet is pleasing to Your eyes."

"You know that I'm not perfect yet You reach for me in love.
You touch me with Your healing hand and cleanse me from above
For even though I'm dressed in sin and death should be the price,
Praise be to God for I now wear the borrowed robes of Christ!"

"You've clothed me in Your righteousness and like the leprous man,
You've broken through the law to cleanse and heal me like a balm.
You warned the leper, tell no soul and let this act suffice
But still he spread the word and so You paid a costly price."

"I see the similarity for at the Cross is seen
The costly price You paid for *me* so *I* could be made clean!
This perfect picture of Your love, my Saviour sacrificed.
My awesome King was manifest within the flesh of Christ."

"So now I may approach Your Throne with confidence secured.
You dealt my sin a deathly blow and in Your sight I'm cured.
Does this forgiveness mean that I behave just like before?
O God forbid and let me praise and love You all the more!"

So when the devil burdens us with guilt and shame too much,
Remember we can seek our King and feel His healing touch.
Though every sin is known to Him and every flaw is seen,
O' child of God arise and hear Christ's blesséd words, "You're clean!"

SCRIPTURE REFERENCES

1 John 1:9

My God

INSPIRATION

I've been learning over time that there are many misconceptions about Jesus Christ. This became apparent to me through having different conversations with people, reading literature, listening to the media or even from watching television programmes with titles such as "The History of Christianity." It seems there are countless misrepresentations of who Jesus is and what it involves to be a follower of Him.

I found myself feeling very saddened and frustrated by this so wanted to write a poem that really drew attention to the differences between "religion" or being "religious" and having a real, loving relationship with the one, true living God. I soon felt inspired to write "My God" as a result.

POEM

My God is not "religion" or rules ordained by man,
Dictation and oppression were not my Saviour's plan.
He did not come to beat us down or scourge us with His wrath.
My God cannot be found within a cold, self-righteous laugh.

My God is not a painting or the image of a Cross,
He doesn't dwell in pictures for my eyes to pour across.
My God is not a building made of mortar, bricks or stone.
He doesn't sit in lavish cloth upon a worldly throne.

He isn't made of gold or brass or any chiseled wood,
He isn't somewhere that I go each week to make me "good."
He's not a guilt-trip or a place I kneel with weary joints
Or turn up just to "show some face" and score some "brownie points."

He's not a stained-glass window deemed as grand in worldly eyes
Or marble statues at whose feet I weep at my demise.
My God is not a ritual or a mantra I recite,
He's not a superstition that I cling to every night.

My God is not embroidered silk to wear with pompous pride,
He's not a box encased in jewels with "Holy Grails" inside.
I don't receive enlightenment igniting wax and wick,
I do not feel more spiritual when doused in incense thick.

My God is not the sections of "religion" I don't mind,
The bits that don't address my sin and leave the truth behind.
I cannot pick and choose the parts to which I'll bow the knee
For He is absolute. My God does *not* bow down to me.

My God is not a crutch I only seek in times of strife,
He's not an empty hope when bad things happen in my life.
My God is not a cult or sect that I was born into,
I've not been brainwashed to believe in things I've not thought through.

My God is not a weakness in my character you see.
My God is Jesus Christ our Lord who died for you and me.
He made Himself of no repute and through the virgin birth,
God manifest Himself in flesh and lived upon the Earth.

Although my God owed nothing, He paid the price for sin.
A perfect, sinless life He led and death could not hold Him!
To reconcile and bridge the gap between our God and man,
Eternal life and fellowship, now *that* was Jesus' plan!

My Lord and God is merciful and faithful to provide.
His love is everlasting and in Him we can abide.
My God is slow to anger and His patience does astound!
The soul who finds their Saviour, what a treasure they have found.

Yet next to Jesus Christ the brightest jewel could not compete!
For diamonds, gems and rubies cannot make your soul complete.
Though worldly gifts and riches in this lifetime may look fair,
When Jesus Christ dwells in your heart this world cannot compare.

My God is full of justice, filled with righteousness and light.
The sacrifice of Jesus shows we're precious in His sight.
His ways are beyond measure, He puts gladness in my heart.
I gaze upon the Heavens, my God's precious work of art.

My God, the one I turned to when burdened with my sin,
The only one to purify and cleanse me from within.
My God who knew my name before the stars were in the sky!
Whose love for me is *endless* and leaves me asking, "Why?"

My Lord, my God how excellent His name is on the Earth!
I sing to Him, the Lord most High who gave me second birth!
My Light and my Salvation, my God is one who saves.
My Refuge and my Glory, He's not one who enslaves.

My God I could not live without for He's my daily bread,
I seek Him in the morning and before I rest my head.
I cherish our communion and His friendship I adore.
I *thrive* in our relationship, He's all I need and more.

He shares my every thought as I recall my highs and lows,
Before a word is on my tongue my God already knows!
My soul waits silently for Him and seeks Him day by day.
My servitude comes from a heart that wishes to obey.

But when I fail and let Him down, when tears will streak my face,
I praise His name remembering that I am saved by grace.
I do not serve my God through guilt, eternal condemnation
For all who come to Christ receive the shield of His salvation!

I love my God with *passion* and I grow in Him each day.
He teaches, guides and comforts me and takes my pain away.
I trust Him for my God relieves my soul in my distress.
His training helps me yield the fruit of peace and righteousness.

Forgiveness, grace and peace, my marvellous God I wish to share!
To think of souls who know Him not, it fills me with despair!
But sadly it's too easy to believe in Satan's lies,
We don't address our flaws and let our sin obstruct our eyes.

We don't like to acknowledge we're *accountable* to God.
We'd rather turn our backs, through utter darkness we will plod.
We turn to our own ways, beyond our sin we cannot see.
My loving God knows how destructive sinful ways can be.

And this is why He sent His Son, the perfect sacrifice.
The punishment that *we* deserved our Saviour paid the price!
It puts my soul in turmoil when I hear of Jesus' death,
It wrenches at my heart to hear my Saviour's dying breath.

To think of all the anguish and the torture *He* endured,
Becoming sin so *our* eternal life might be secured!
What drove my God to darkest depths? What fuelled this motivation?
The noblest reason above all, God's love for His creation.

For every sin committed, they're now paid for, every one.
God took His mighty wrath and poured it out upon His Son.
We don't deserve forgiveness! We don't deserve His grace!
And yet through Jesus Christ He put Himself there in our place.

My God who took the Cross died with forgiveness in His prayer
And that is why no gold or cloth or statue can compare!
I owe my Saviour everything, my soul before was black.
He bought me at a price and so I gladly give it back.

And this is not from protocol or rules of pomp and air.
I choose my God through *love*, I pray you see the difference there.
I know that some find faith and joy in-keeping with tradition
But don't mistake my living God for cold, man-made "religion."

Instead of pointing us to Christ, our never changing Rock
It leads us to a legalistic, pious stumbling block.
This does not represent my God! It's wickedness, deceit!
Perhaps selfish ambition or perhaps it's vain conceit.

For many times in history and even to this day
Are cruel and wicked acts by "men of God" or so they say
But this is *not* my Saviour! This is *not* done in His name!
These men will stand before their God and recognise their shame.

The Kingdom of my God cannot be won with blade or rifle
For not in *His* name do they fight, or kill, oppress or stifle.
Their *greed* and their *ambition* mean their hearts t'wards Him are locked
But He sees all, the war is *His* and God will *not* be mocked.

Our outer image cannot trick my God who knows our minds.
Imagine Jesus' grief if false belief is all He finds.
He bought us at a price for Jesus came to liberate,
He came to give us life and joy and not to suffocate.

With Jesus we are challenged and our lives may bear much fruit!
"Religion" means we settle for a morbid substitute.
No longer is He broken and still hanging on the Tree,
He rose again now we rejoice for all eternity!

He does not ask that we remain within perpetual sorrow,
He wants us to rejoice with Him and see a bright tomorrow!
My God is what is missing! My God who died for me!
He paid the price for sin that all mankind could be set free!

For each and every person is a part of His creation,
We're living proof of God's delight and vast imagination.
Yes on our knees, confess, repent then rise up and rejoice!
For Hallelujah! We can hear our risen Saviour's voice!

And so I give my heart to Him for now my soul can thrive
For Jesus Christ, my Lord and God is very much alive!
Salvation is His gift, for those who seek Him He preserves.
Let every tongue confess His name! Our worship He deserves.

My God is not "religion," He's my everlasting King.
He's my morning and my evening and He's my everything.
My God who chose the Cross, the path to Calvary He trod
So all the world may know the love of Jesus Christ, my God.

SCRIPTURE REFERENCES

Acts 17:22-31

AFTERWORD

Not long after I shared this poem on my website I had an e-mail from a young woman saying that she had been raised in a family that went to Church but that she had never heard anyone talk about Jesus in the way that the poem speaks about Him. She explained that her idea of God had been that He was a very un-knowable, distant figure but felt that after reading this poem she really wanted to know Jesus in the same way as I did.

We arranged to meet up and after a few conversations over a short space of time she felt led to give her heart and life to the Lord. Years on and she's still walking faithfully with her Saviour and I'm so grateful that the Lord chose to use this poem to speak to her heart and soul in a personal way. I pray it can continue to be a witness for the wonderful, personal Saviour I know and love!

Even When I Sleep

My inspiration for this poem came from a very strange event that happened to me late one night. I was in the middle of having a nightmare and felt the Lord stirring me and making me aware of the fact that I needed to wake up. I've been aware of Jesus "rescuing" me from unpleasant dreams several times in the past but as I started to come around I discovered to my horror that I couldn't actually move any part of my body! I couldn't even speak or make a noise and felt like I was being pinned to my bed! It was as if there was a huge pressure pushing down on my chest and arms and it felt like it was spreading down my whole body. I knew that if I didn't get it to stop then the sensation was going to keep getting worse and more frightening.

In my hazy state of paralysis and panic the only thing I could think to do was cry out to Jesus for help, which of course is also the best thing to do in any situation! In my heart and mind I cried out into the night three words, "Jesus! Help me!"

In the same second that I called out to Him the heavy, crushing feeling that was spreading down my body like water completely lifted off me and evaporated into thin air. Suddenly I felt like I could breathe again and was very grateful to find the control of my limbs had returned. Feeling quite frightened by the whole thing I gave my husband Jan a shake and sluggishly muttered something along the lines of "I had a nightmare!" Now if I'm woken up in the night I'm pretty much like the Grinch! Thankfully Jan is far more gracious and he turned over, pulled me into a cuddle and I promptly went back to sleep.

The next day I was thinking, "What on Earth was that about?" I figured I'd make the most of the internet facility we have these days and so naturally decided to Google it! I discovered that what I had experienced the night before sounded exactly like something called

"Sleep Paralysis." Apparently it's caused by a chemical released by the brain during the REM (rapid eye movement) section of sleep to make the body inactive and relaxed so that we don't physically live out our dreams. If the chemical kicks in too early as the person falls asleep or doesn't wear off quickly enough as they wake up it can leave them feeling like they're paralysed for a time. It's very unpleasant as I discovered but doesn't cause any long-term damage thankfully!

I do also feel that what happened to me that night definitely had an element of spiritual warfare to it. It felt extremely dark and oppressive and very much like an attack so it just got me thinking about how vulnerable we are as humans when we go to sleep and by contrast how powerful Jesus is. He never sleeps and this experience really showed me that He never takes His eyes away from His children.

Of course I already knew that God never goes to sleep but to go through such an event and discover first hand that no matter what time of day it is and what condition your mind may be in, when you call out to Jesus He's always there and able to help. His power knows no boundaries and He's attentive to every minute of our lives, even when we sleep! That's definitely a God worth sharing with others.

POEM

Even when I sleep I know my Saviour's always there,
When nightmares fill my mind with fear I know He hears my prayer.
Though vulnerable with no defence to claim or call my own
I know that even when I sleep my Saviour's on His Throne.

A misty world of hazy thoughts, a maze of dark and light.
I shall not fret or be afraid of terrors in the night
For Jesus is my Refuge and my dreams He oversees,
His presence in my sleep is like a cool, refreshing breeze.

He chases every eerie and pernicious, frightening thought
Or images so terrible I know are not of God.
Though sleep may make my mind just like a cave to be explored
I know I venture nowhere without Christ, my Sovereign Lord.

For even when I sleep I know His eyes are watching me,
We walk disjointed paths that only He and I can see.
So when the visions of the night are dark and bring despair
I call out to my Saviour and He proves He's always there.

His power knows no boundaries and sleep can challenge not
My awesome God who rescues me when dreams are tense and fraught.
He reaches my subconscious as He sees my fears increase,
He gently reassures my soul and brings me restful peace.

It's comforting to know from Jesus Christ I cannot stray;
To my all-seeing, watchful God the night will shine like day.
When turbid dreams grow sinister He cuts right through the dim
For dark and light are both alike and just the same to Him.

With broken thoughts I venture through the mystic midnight lands
But even when I sleep I know my life is in His hands.
His Spirit joins me in the depths wherever I may roam
And if I stray and wander far my Saviour brings me home.

He never takes His eyes from those whose hearts belong to Him,
He guards them with His Spirit, with His mighty Cherubim.
His eyes go to and fro across the Earth for hearts to reap;
What privilege is mine to serve a God who doesn't sleep!

So even when I sleep I wish to share the Gospel news,
I dream of pointing souls to Christ, the Saviour there to choose.
Within the dark of night my heart's desire is the same,
To point the lost t'wards Jesus and bring glory to His name.

I play the role of supplicant, emotions feel extreme
As echoes of real life begin to permeate my dream.
My sleeping limbs lie dormant while recovering their strength
But mind and soul engage in sharing Jesus Christ at length.

In dreams I speak with confidence, with urgency so strong,
Convincing souls of Satan's lies, to see the right from wrong.
Within surreal encounters I engage in godly talk,
Encouraging each soul to seek the narrow path to walk.

I fervently describe the loss that Jesus Christ endured
That we might have redemption and eternal life secured.
He brought us out of darkness through His sacrificial pains.
He freed the slaves of sin and death for Jesus broke the chains!

Our perfect Lord who knew no fault endured horrendous loss
For every sin was nailed with Christ upon the Roman Cross.
He took the judgment and the wrath that wasn't His to take;
The Son of God was crucified for His beloved's sake.

Yes even in my sleep this sober truth I wish to share,
In Heaven we have righteous robes of purest white to wear!
But this is not from efforts of our own that have sufficed,
We have a place prepared for us and through the blood of Christ.

I speak about the love of God and pointing to the truth
I beg and plead that they'd believe, let *Jesus* be their proof!
I ask that they would choose the God who'll set their spirit free,
The Lord of my salvation for He did the same for me.

My dreams at night inspire me to live for Jesus' sake,
They give me confidence to do the same when I awake.
Though deep within the world of sleep I cannot take control
I rest in knowing Jesus has His hand upon my soul.

So even when I sleep I'm not beyond my Saviour's touch,
There is no height or depth or any distance that's too much.
He only has to speak before the darkness tries to hide!
Forever my Companion, in His safety I'll abide.

His mighty arms protectively surround my sleeping form,
As minutes tick throughout the dark His presence keeps me warm.
I never face the night alone, a truth so dear to keep.
My faithful Jesus by my side, even when I sleep.

SCRIPTURE REFERENCES

Psalm 34:15; Psalm 119:55

As Long As I Live

Inspiration

One day I was reading through Psalm 104 and when I came to verse 33 it really jumped out at me. It reads,

"I will sing to the Lord as long as I live;
I will sing praise to my God while I have my being."

I thought this was a beautiful Scripture and I felt that the rhythm and sentiment of the verse lent itself perfectly well for a poem! Within a matter of seconds I found myself writing "As Long As I Live."

Poem

As long as I live I will sing the name Jesus,
While I still have my being I'll offer Him praise.
May my soul's meditation be sweet in His presence
And my spirit be glad in the Lord all my days.

As long as I live may I do of His pleasure
And keep His commandments with reverence and fear.
May I always consider the Lord who is awesome,
The one to be worshipped, the one to revere.

He appointed the moon and declared different seasons,
Created the hills and put oceans in place.
He stamped His existence through all His dominion
That man would cry out, evermore seek His face.

May I pause to consider the hands that have made me,
The eyes that could see the frame still yet to come.
For deep in the Earth my Lord skilfully wrought me
With days that were fashioned when yet there were none.

As long as I live let my heart call upon Him,
Make known to the peoples His deeds great and small.
May I speak of His wonders, His works strong and mighty,
He is Lord of creation and Lord over all.

As long as I live I shall speak of His goodness
If He bless me with riches or take them away.
For I know in His Son I am clean and accepted,
Escaping His wrath when I face Judgment Day.

May I always remember the day at Golgotha,
The place of the skull and the sufferings of Christ.
The curtain was torn and the pearly gates opened
Thanks to the love of the Lamb sacrificed.

As long as I live I will speak of His mercy,
Let me always remember He saved me by grace.
May I live with the knowledge and joy that in Heaven
My soul will be greeted by Christ's warm embrace.

I will contemplate how He removed my transgressions,
He took them as far as the East is from West!
Praise God O my soul and find peace in the promise
That Jesus is sovereign and always knows best.

For my life is a vapour so swift and so fleeting,
The passing of time acts as proof to confirm
My days have been numbered and though my heart's beating,
From dust I was made and to dust I'll return.

Give thanks to the Lord for His statutes and counsel,
For wisdom and knowledge belong in His palm.
To know that His judgments are righteous and holy,
My lips sing with praises, my heart with a psalm.

As long as I live I will seek His approval
And thank the Lord daily for covering my sin.
For God has established His Throne in the Heavens,
Forgiveness and mercy lie solely with Him.

Each day of my life may I share His communion
For God knows me better than I know myself.
Such knowledge so high that I cannot attain it!
His fellowship means so much more than great wealth.

With every new dawn may I seek strength from Jesus,
Find comfort and solace when trials are rife.
Dominion and power belong to my Saviour,
Alone He's the Fortress and Rock of my life.

As long as I live I will speak of one Saviour,
I'll testify only to one sovereign King.
No God was before Him nor shall there be after.
Salvation belongs to those under *His* wing.

Each day that I live may I give thanks to Jesus
For blessings so cherished, too many to count.
For family and friends and for treasure in Heaven,
For riches He's added against my account.

As long as I live may I give God the glory,
The service and honour and praise He is due.
Without Him I'm nothing for He who is holy
Deserves my heart's worship in all that I do.

As long as I live may l write of my Saviour.
My time and my efforts to Him I will give.
I'll share with the world the one true Creator.
I will serve the Lord Jesus as long as I live.

SCRIPTURE REFERENCES

Psalm 119:112

Unto You

I'm sure many Christians know what a struggle it can be working in a very secular environment. A job in Performing Arts can certainly bring it's challenges as well as blessings. However, even if we work within the Church or an area of ministry, there will always be battles to face and spiritual warfare to endure. After all, this world is not our home!

It was during a particularly troublesome time at work when I was being persecuted for my faith that I wrote "Unto You." This poem is really a prayer that came from my heart one evening as I was giving the concerns and frustrations I was experiencing in my workplace over to the Lord.

Poem

Unto You sovereign Lord I commit all my effort,
I will not look to man for reward and acclaim.
My time and my skills are gifts You have given,
Let me always remember I serve in Your name.

Unto You my Father I give every struggle,
Keep my spirit and heart in the place that is right.
When I'm weary and feel I'm devoid of all motive,
Turn the sweat of my brow into beads of delight.

Unto You righteous God I commit all injustice,
Let me never be burdened by hardships unfair.
For You see my labour, I know You are sovereign,
You won't permit trials that my soul cannot bear.

Unto You faithful Lord I commit my frustration,
When opinions may differ and conflict is found.
May I act in a way that's reflective of Jesus,
Let my flesh be restrained that Your grace may abound.

May I never respond in a way that is lofty
For pompous and prideful are not what You are.
You're the Father of mercies and God of all comfort.
Help me represent You Lord, my bright Morning Star.

Unto You awesome God I commit every battle
For You are my strength in this troublesome time.
Let my fiery tongue be restrained by Your Spirit,
May Your wisdom be known, Your discernment be mine.

Unto You precious God may I point people daily,
In my actions and attitude, words and in deed.
Let my life be a witness in spite of my failures,
May they see in my conduct the Saviour they need.

Let me not be surprised when surroundings are hostile
Lest my soul be discouraged from running the race.
Help me lay aside sin and to run with endurance,
May the Gospel of Christ be my cause and my case.

I ask gentle Lord that You help me stay focused,
I'm here for Your service, my life is not mine.
Keep my sights on the task that You've laid out before me.
Help me pray just like Jesus, "Not *my* will but Thine."

May I give You my worship for all I accomplish,
Let correction be mine if *my* glory I seek
For my body is Yours as my reasonable service.
Keep my soul ever humble, my attitude meek.

May Your glory shine forth from my fibre and being,
Let my works sing Your praises in all that I do.
My reason and purpose, my life's very meaning
I now recommit, dearest Lord, unto You.

SCRIPTURE REFERENCES

Colossians 3:23-24

Christmas Tree

It was the week before Christmas in 2010 and my Pastor gave a teaching on the Sunday morning about two trees. He compared the tree in the garden of Eden to the Tree that Jesus Christ was nailed to. It was a wonderful teaching and I found myself being inspired to write a poem also comparing two trees but for my poem I decided I would compare the well known image of the Christmas tree with the less romantic vision of the Cross. I really enjoyed writing this poem and I don't think I'll ever look at a Christmas tree in the same way again!

Poem

O' Christmas tree, O' Christmas tree. A blessèd sight for all to see!
With coloured beads and lights that dance, you put me in a
festive trance!
I marvel at your needled arms parading red and golden charms.
With tinsel draped and set in place you stand above the gifts with grace.

O' Christmas tree, O' Christmas tree. A truly splendid sight to me!
You join us through December days and bring us joy with
Christmas ways.
You help us mark the time of year, a special month we hold so dear.
The 25th of cold December, the date of birth that we remember.

You chase away the winter gloom with fragrant scents that fill the room.
As light reflects off baubles round a warmer heart is often found.
You get my senses all a-twitter, crowned on top by star of glitter!
You are indeed O' Christmas tree a blessèd sight for all to see!

Yet though you're favourite for the season there is a Tree with
deeper reason.
A Tree where at it's roots you'll find a bridge was built for all mankind.
A Tree where love and justice meet, where rusty nails pierced hands
and feet.
A Tree of torture, death and pain. The Tree where Jesus Christ was slain.

O' how you differ Christmas tree from this, the Cross of Calvary.
Embellished *not* by pretty charms as ropes restrained His legs and arms.
Submitted to the Father's rod as Christ endured the wrath of God
For there the Saviour's flesh was torn, *this* Tree displayed a crown
of thorns.

You're far removed O' Christmas tree, the Cross does not stand prettily.
Aesthetically it won't appease, this Tree cannot be viewed with ease
For there I see my suffering King with vulgar crowds surrounding Him.
The taunting priests who mocked Him so, the King of Jews they would
not know.

To see my humble Saviour die, it tempts me to avert my eye
But there upon His bloodied face I see from God His gift of grace.
The Father's love for us revealed, by Jesus' stripes we all are healed!
Forgiveness flows there like a flood because of Jesus' crimson blood.

Though violence reigned and sin was rife, Christ secured eternal life.
Let Satan's lies and trickery not keep me from Redemption's Tree.
The Cross bore Jesus as it's fruit, I'll taste and see the Lord is good!
For God commands I eat of Him in order to be freed from sin.

And now through Christ I'm made alive, in Him my heart and soul can
thrive.
His judgment I no longer face, His Christmas gift to me is *grace*!
So though the Cross is dark and cruel, to me this sight is beautiful
For there the Saviour bought my pass to dwell with Him in Heaven
at last.

O' Cross of Christ, Redeeming Tree, where God can meet me readily.
Though planted at the hand of man your purpose served the
Father's plan
For sin was slain and debts were paid and peace for God and man
was made.
Though changing seasons yet remain, this work of Christ will stay
the same.

O' Christmas Tree, *real* Christmas Tree. The one where Jesus died
for me.
You point us to the meaning true, that Christmas Day then leads
to you.
Please keep our eyes from gifts we get and to the Cross, lest we forget.
You are indeed O' Christmas Tree, a blessèd sight for all to see.

SCRIPTURE REFERENCES

Philippians 2:8; 1 Corinthians 11:23-25

NOT A DAY MORE

INSPIRATION

"Not A Day More" is a very emotive poem. My inspiration came from a situation my family and I had been going through for a few years by the time of writing it in 2011.

My belovèd Grandmother suffered from Alzheimer's disease before she was called home to be with her Saviour in 2015. Leading up to this time we had been witnessing her succumb more and more to the symptoms of this condition. Sadly we were learning first-hand how upsetting and painful this process is for everyone involved.

The situation reached a particularly low point in January of 2011 and as a result I found myself on my knees crying out to the Lord on behalf of my Gran, almost out of desperation for her. I was wondering why things had been allowed to become as bad as they were.

Now I know that the Lord didn't owe me any answers as I sat there asking Him "Why? Why? Why?" so I feel that it was thanks to His grace that He gently spoke to my heart on the matter. He reminded me that He is God and that He's a good God. He then brought it to my mind that He is sovereign and everything He has permitted into our lives is for a reason. With Jesus we can get through anything that comes our way, not because of our own strength but because of His.

I also felt the Lord reminding me that only He can see the full picture and purpose of each situation in life and that He is a God who is worthy to be trusted. This really helped to still my soul before Him and I found myself having the peace of God that transcends all understanding, the peace that only Jesus Christ can give.

Having gone on this emotional journey with the Lord I felt inspired to write "Not A Day More."

POEM

Why when there's anguish? Why when there's turmoil?
Why when her mind cannot call on Your name?
Why when her days are not clear or remembered?
Why put her soul through such torment and pain?

Why let her linger when eyes are so vacant?
A body so tired is surely a sign
That purpose and meaning have all but departed.
What heartache and sorrow to see such decline.

Why when it seems she has left us already?
Confusion and upset are clouding her mind.
The person we knew is now but a shadow.
A fearful, frail shell has been left behind.

Before dark descended we know that she chose You,
Before all the troubles the illness creates.
We know Your salvation was wholly accepted.
Why when we know that Your Heaven awaits?

Oh how my heart wishes that things could be different,
I wish to my soul that there were no goodbyes.
If I had my way she would stay here forever
But time waits for nothing, time no one defies.

So now we must witness our loved one grow distant.
The curse of this world causes deep down to cry,
"How long must we wait for our Saviour's arrival?"
Why do You linger Lord? Why Jesus? Why?

But I must be still and remember Your goodness,
Find comfort and peace as I pray in Your name.
Recalling the words of Paul the Apostle,
"To live is Christ and to die is gain."

For You are our God and You're filled with compassion.
Your judgments are righteous, Your purposes wise
For each of Your children has days You've appointed.
Each moment has meaning when seen through *Your* eyes.

For I cannot see the big picture like You do.
I don't know Your reasons or purpose or plan
For sustaining the days when it seems they are futile.
There's comfort in knowing her life's in Your palm.

Our affliction on Earth is here for a moment
And works in us glory with an eternal weight.
You renew our hearts every day that we're given.
Your timing is perfect and never too late.

For who knows the secrets of each life like You do
With unresolved issues we try to forget?
Perhaps You are using this time to heal heartache
Or speaking to souls who don't know You yet.

For we mustn't lean on our own understanding
But trust in Your wisdom and Fatherly care.
Perhaps You are teaching us spiritual lessons,
Be it love or compassion or time spent in prayer.

Whatever the reasons, we know You are sovereign.
To this we submit with all reverence and fear.
We long for the day when all sorrow is ended
And our Lord Jesus Christ wipes away every tear.

As we wait for that day may we live with the knowledge
That every new breath is a gift that's from You.
Our days here on Earth are precious and fleeting,
May we use our time wisely in all that we do.

But when will the trials of life be concluded?
When will we finally see Heaven's door?
When our lives have fulfilled every day You've appointed.
When Your work is completed and not a day more.

SCRIPTURE REFERENCES

2 Corinthians 4:16-18

THE ENEMY

INSPIRATION

I wrote "The Enemy" because there seems to be quite a common opinion these days that God is the enemy of mankind and of Planet Earth. I often hear news reporters describing hurricanes and natural disasters as "Acts of God." I find myself wondering why it's considered an act of God. I don't hear reports thanking Him for the many sunny days we get throughout the year so why is it only the bad weather that God gets the credit for?

In this world where society denies the existence of God so often, it's suddenly acceptable for God to exist but only for the sole purpose that we can blame Him for something! This never sits very well with me and I find myself wanting to ask the question, "Why do you think God would want to bring such destruction and suffering on the very world that He created?"

To believe that God is "the enemy" is to believe in a lie from the devil. I think that Satan wants us to think that God is our enemy to keep us from discovering our loving, forgiving Saviour and to prevent us from receiving our salvation.

It's very clear to see that this world is descending more and more rapidly into utter chaos and unrest just as the Bible always said it would. The Bible also says that Jesus is coming back and will bring an end to pain and suffering once and for all but that promise brings some questions for each and every person. Questions such as, where do I stand with Jesus? Where do I personally stand with God? Do I consider Him my friend or do I think of Him as my enemy? Have I made Him my enemy either by blaming Him for the problems of the world or by just downright refusing to believe in His existence? Will the day that He returns be the best day of my life or the worst day I've ever had?

The outcome of that day will be the result of who we have spent our lives believing to be "the enemy."

I really want to encourage people in these uncertain and frightening times not to blame God for all the problems in the world and not to see them as an excuse to point the finger and feel like we have a right to be angry with Him. Rather, let these circumstances be the very reason we get on our knees before Him and ask for forgiveness. We need to make sure we know when that day comes and Jesus returns to this Earth to claim His bride, we're on the right side and we know exactly where we stand with Jesus. May we feel the safety, security and peace of mind knowing that we stand with Him!

POEM

God is not the enemy. God is not to blame.
When anger burns within your soul don't curse my Saviour's name
For He is not the one who causes raging wars and strife.
He's not the one responsible for heartache in your life.

It's clear to see this life is filled with suffering and pain
But please do not be quick to say that *God's* the one to blame.
So often I hear blasphemies when things don't go our way
But tell me, do you thank the Lord for *blessings* in your day?

We don't acknowledge God when taking credit for success
But then we feel a right to wrath if life gives any less!
Indignantly we shout at God as if He owes us more,
The God we didn't talk to or want to know before.

Or when we see injustices through television screens,
In disbelief we look to God to vent frustrated screams.
Imploring Him as if He really needs us to advise
But nothing happens on this Earth that can evade His eyes.

For God created Planet Earth and said "Let there be light!"
He put the sun and moon in place to give us day and night.
He filled the Earth abundantly with animals and food,
He looked at all He'd made and He declared that it was good.

So why would God find any joy destroying His creation?
To see what it's become must be a source of great frustration.
Instead of dwelling peacefully where harmony is found,
We battle to exist where sin and wickedness abound.

It's like a stained-glass window full of beauty and design
That then becomes the victim of a wicked, evil crime.
It's like a hateful vandal throwing rubble, rocks and sticks.
So who should we be angry with? The one who's throwing bricks!

So let's reveal the one to blame, it's time to name and shame him!
"Prince of the air," "the father of lies," also known as Satan.
He's the one responsible for this dark world of sin
But also sharing in the blame is man's rebellion.

We disobeyed and ate the fruit, betrayed the human race.
Dominion went to Satan and now *he* reigns in our place.
You only have to watch the news and hear of troubles there
To see, no need for horror films, we're living a nightmare!

Cancer, aids and pestilence, murder, rape and death.
Illnesses that steal young life, replaced by dying breath.
Famines, floods and hurricanes, a natural disaster;
Destroying human life, at this the devil is a master.

A myriad of ways to try and ruin God's creation.
His actions fuelled by hatred seek to wipe out every nation.
The greatest trick of all of course, a lie been told before.
Convince mankind to kill himself, disguised as "Holy War."

Yes those who say they "fight for God" while shooting people dead
Are blinded by the enemy and fight for him instead.
But God predicted all these things and said they would be signs.
Like falling leaves in autumn, it's the coming of "End Times."

So many sorrows we will see, of this there is no doubt.
The devil knows his reign is short, his time is running out.
For Jesus Christ will come again and bring an end to pain.
Each day we long a little more for Christ's eternal reign.

Behold He's coming quickly for His promises are true!
And when He comes the final time how will Christ find you?
Will you be on your knees in prayer or giving Him your praise?
Perhaps He'll find a faithful servant living out their days.

Will Jesus find you deep in sorrow, trusting more in Him?
Or find a thankful heart for all the blessings pouring in?
When Christ returns, will it be a moment full of strife
Or the moment you've been waiting for with ernest all your life?

Will you be found rejecting God and living for yourself
With hedonistic motives, craving worldly goods and wealth?
Will Jesus find your name inscribed on His eternal list
Or did you live your life to curse His name and shake your fist?

The sides are "Good and Evil, God and Satan, peace and strife"
And each of us must choose who we will live to serve in life.
The devil will convince you that it's *you* who's in control
But understand it's warfare, there's a battle for your soul.

Please don't believe in Satan's lies, there's far too much at stake.
Don't think that God is powerless for that's a huge mistake.
So when we see deep suffering and cruelty at it's worst,
Remember there's no pain we feel that Christ did not know first.

God is not the enemy. God is not to blame.
When troubles seem to get too much don't curse my Saviour's name.
He had every right to leave us in our self inflicted mess,
We forfeited our bond with God, the cause of our distress.

But even though we disowned God and turned our backs on Him,
Our humble Saviour loved us still and paid the price for sin.
He dwells up in the Heavens where our access was denied
So if God *was* the enemy then Jesus *wouldn't* have died!

He never would have come to Earth to show the Father's love,
Revealing His desire for our fellowship above.
So no one can accuse Him of abandoning mankind
For Jesus *died* for us and greater love you will not find.

Don't pit yourself against Him, it's a foolish thing to do
For when life gets too much He'll give you strength to see you through.
He's worthy to be trusted and to know God as your friend,
You'll see we're in His hands as this world's coming to it's end.

God is not the enemy. God is not to blame.
When Satan fills your head with lies don't curse your Saviour's name.
Find peace and comfort in God's strength, with Him you will
stand firm.
May faith in Christ unite us as we wait for His return.

SCRIPTURE REFERENCES

John 3:16-17

AFTERWORD

I received an e-mail one evening from a lady I didn't know saying she had just been reading this poem. She explained that she had been brought up in a home where she and her sibling were taken to Church each Sunday but then had to endure terrible abuse in the home every other day of the week. This had left her with the idea that God must approve of the abuse and must be ok with the way she was being treated. The idea that someone could go to Church and still behave that way meant that she linked this awful behaviour with God.

The woman went on to tell me that the poem had turned all her ideas about God upside down and that she finally understood who was really to blame for the awful situation. She explained that she had been angry with God for years but now could see that Jesus loved her and wasn't the source of her heartache at all. Thankfully she went on to give her heart to Jesus and allowed the Lord to start repairing the damage that had been done in her early years.

I hope and pray this poem may help others really understand why there is so much suffering in life. I've used these words many times when I've been chatting to people if they bring up the subject of "suffering." It can often be a touchy topic and many times people use the subject of "suffering" as an excuse not to believe in God. Rather than getting into a debate I often just ask if I can share a poem with them and send it to them to read in their own time. I find this gives people a chance to hear the truth without feeling the need to be on the defensive. I think people are much more willing to be open to other ideas when they're in private and can mull things over with no pressure on them.

An Atheist colleague of mine once said to me after I shared the poem with him, "I don't agree with your viewpoint but now I understand it and respect your argument." We never know how God will speak to someone's heart but I just feel that there's so much heartache in the world that people really need to hear some answers and hear that God loves them! The answers are all right there in the Bible, we just have to be open-minded enough to listen.

No One But Jesus

Inspiration

This is quite a simple little poem but I felt inspired to write it having heard the words "No one but Jesus" spoken during the Church service one week. I thought they made a great title for a poem and so started writing straight away.

I began to think about some of the wonderful benefits of knowing Jesus Christ as my personal Saviour and also why He is so different from anyone else who has ever walked the face of the Earth. I was considering why He can claim things that no one else can claim. When it comes to paying for the sins of the world, the Resurrection and eternal life, no one but Jesus will do!

Poem

Who could endure that torturous Cross?
No one but Jesus will do.
Who could withstand such harrowing loss?
No one but Jesus will do.

For who loved sinners enough to face
The wrath of God and to take their place?
Who could bestow such amazing grace?
No one but Jesus will do.

Who lived a life that was sinless and pure?
No one but Jesus will do.
Who could provide all mankind with a cure?
No one but Jesus will do.

Who had the strength to defeat death's door?
No one succeeding and no one before.
To think of my Saviour it makes my heart soar.
No one but Jesus will do.

Who can I turn to when troubles abound?
No one but Jesus will do.
Who provides comfort when words can't be found?
No one but Jesus will do.

Whose truth can I lean on when trials cut deep?
Whose words reassure me with peace I can keep?
A harvest of treasures for my heart to reap!
No one but Jesus will do.

To whom am I grateful when blessings pour in?
No one but Jesus will do.
Who to thank daily for covering my sin?
No one but Jesus will do.

Who gives me a reason in life to rejoice?
My soul sings His praises, my heart knows His voice.
The Lord called my spirit to make the right choice!
And no one but Jesus will do.

So whose is the name that I share with my friends?
No one's but Jesus' will do.
Who can give hope to us when this life ends?
No one but Jesus will do.

Who humbled Himself to save you and me?
Who rescued our souls and set us all free?
Who shall I love for eternity?
No one but Jesus will do.

SCRIPTURE REFERENCES

Matthew 11:28-30

BORN THIS WAY

INSPIRATION

Discussing the issue of sin can often be very difficult and uncomfortable. It's part of our nature to want to defend ourselves so being able to recognise and admit to our faults and flaws challenges us to the very core. It is however an essential part to receiving God's forgiveness and everlasting life because without acknowledging our sin and repenting of it, we can never be accepted into His presence.

In society these days there seems to be a common opinion that "right and wrong" are subjective and there are no moral absolutes. Many times I've heard people trying to defend or excuse their sin by using the statement, "I was born this way" or words to that effect. I've heard it said, "If there is a God then He made me this way" or "It's not my fault I have a fiery temper, I was born this way!"

The world teaches us that there probably is no God and even if there is, we don't have to acknowledge Him. Just live life for ourselves in any way that we feel is right, do what we think will make us happy and don't ever apologise for being the way we are. After all, we were born this way!

The Bible teaches us something very different however. It teaches us that there definitely is a God and He created us but did not create the sin in us. He is our Maker but as a result of our rebellion we are all born with a sinful nature. The Bible shows us that despite our rebellion, He loves us dearly but hates our sin and because He is a righteous God He cannot accept our sin into His presence.

Thankfully because of God's amazing love for us, He paid for our sin by sending His Son Jesus to the Cross where He took the punishment that we deserved. As a result we all have the free-will to choose whether or not to accept God's gift of grace through this sacrifice. The Bible also tells us that one day we will all stand before God to give an account of our lives. We will either do this with Jesus as our loving Saviour or as our righteous Judge, depending on our response to the Cross of Christ.

To stay stubbornly attached to our sin and refuse God's free gift of grace is a tragedy for this life and the next. Christ has dealt with this issue for us and there is no sin in the world that He didn't pay for on the Cross. There is no sin that His power cannot help us overcome. All we have to do is recognise our sin for what it is and stop loving it more than God.

To believe "I was born this way" is a feasible excuse for sin is to believe in a lie of Satan. I felt inspired to write a poem that opposed this lie and pointed instead to the truth.

POEM

"I was born this way!" I hear people say
"So don't you dare tell me there comes Judgement Day!
There's no sin in me as far as I see
And I make my own rules up to benefit me."

"Don't tell me what's right in *your* narrow sight
For *I* don't believe He's the Truth or the Light!
If *you* think it's true it applies then to you
But I won't accept being told what to do."

"I see myself wise in my own pair of eyes,
From God and His presence I sever all ties.
But if He *should* exist then I shall resist
And in His direction I now shake my fist."

"My life is my own so if God's on His Throne
You can tell Him from me He'd best leave me alone.
I don't *want* to change, my life rearrange.
They'd all think I'm crazy or gone a bit strange."

"Besides I'm quite good! When I'm in the right mood.
So I use the odd word that's a little bit crude.
And so what if I lie or make people cry?
There are much worse than me! No one's going to die!"

"You can beg, plead and nudge but I never will budge.
Of my actions and life I will be my own judge!
Besides who can tell if there's really a hell?
I'll meet all my friends there and get on quite well!"

"And God makes no mistakes with the people He makes.
So I'll be true to myself for that's all it takes.
If I sin every day, well He made me that way!
And I think I'm great so what more can I say?"

"No there's nothing I lack and I'm on the right track.
I was born this way and I'll never look back.
And I don't want to hear there's a God I should fear!
I'm king of my life! Do I make myself clear?"

How it saddens my heart and tears me apart
To hear that from Jesus some choose to depart.
Yes God makes no mistakes with the people He makes
But your sin is not His so just put on the brakes!

It's because of the fall that sin dwells in us all.
Between God and man sits rebellion's wall.
So we *all* have to face that our sin's a disgrace
And thank the Lord Jesus for His saving grace!

We may not want to hear there's a God we should fear
But there is, He's our Maker who loves us so dear.
So we cannot excuse the sins that we choose,
Denial is merely a tactic we use.

I'm no better than you for I'm sinful too
But all found in Jesus have now been made new.
So please open your eyes and see Satan's lies.
From him and *his* presence please sever all ties!

Now please understand I wish not to sound grand
But long only to see that you take the Lord's hand.
Christ died on the Tree to *save* you and me!
He paid off our debt and set us all free.

Removing our sin so that we could come in
And dwell in His Kingdom forever with Him.
For those who won't kneel, His wrath they will feel
For they have rejected the one who can heal.

They can't say they knew not or that they just forgot
As they give an account when receiving their lot.
God's shown us the truth and He's given us proof,
We can never accuse Him of being aloof.

There's so much you could lose if you will not choose
The one sent from Heaven to bring us good news!
You could learn of His love and be blessed from above,
Receive His forgiveness as white as a dove.

For those who will trust in the God who is just
Will all be found blameless when flesh turns to dust.
His Word does confirm that this truth will stand firm
But He never will force you to love in return.

For He came not to preach but to save and to teach,
The gift of free-will Jesus never will breach.
Should you long for His voice and to make the right choice
You'll find freedom and make hosts of Heaven rejoice!

We *were* born this way just as you say
So we have to repent for there comes Judgement Day.
Dear friend I will pray that you heed what I say.
Choose Jesus and be *born again* a new way!

SCRIPTURE REFERENCES

John 3:1-7

ONE WAY

I've heard it said many times that to say there is only one way to Heaven is far too "narrow-minded." If someone developed a cure for cancer however I can't imagine cancer sufferers declining the offer simply because there was only one option. I think everyone would just be incredibly grateful that there was a cure and that there was an option at all! So it is with the sin issue. We're all under a death sentence as a result of suffering from the deadly disease called sin and there's only one cure for it, Christ's sacrifice on the Cross. As John 3:16-17 declares,

"For God so loved the world that He gave His only begotten Son, that whoever believes in Him should not perish but have everlasting life. For God did not send His Son into the world to condemn the world, but that the world through Him might be saved."

The Bible also tells us in Romans 6:23 that the wages of sin is death so if we won't die to our sin in life then we will die for our sin. If we won't slay sin then sin will slay us. Either we will pay for our sins in eternity or we can accept that Jesus paid for them on our behalf when He died on the Cross. One way or another our sin has to be paid for. This may not be a comfortable topic of discussion but it's an important one. As Jesus says in John 14:6,

"I am the way, the truth and the life. No one comes to the Father except through Me."

This may be "narrow-minded" to some people but Jesus never claimed the way to Heaven would be broad. He says in Matthew 7:13-14,

"Enter by the narrow gate; for wide is the gate and broad is the way that leads to destruction, and there are many who go in by it. Because narrow is the gate and difficult is the way which leads to life, and there are few who find it."

When we view our sin situation in the correct way we'll realise that to keep viewing a "narrow" way as a negative thing is foolish. A narrow corridor that offers escape out of a burning building is better than no escape at all.

My poem covers many topics and different points of view so I hope that it can ultimately help us understand God's love towards us. Thanks to His grace and mercy He didn't leave us alone with the consequences of our sin. I pray our hearts can come to understand more about the sacrifice God has made on our behalf to provide us with a way to spend eternity with Him!

POEM

So many different points of view and angles to perceive
So how do we decide on which "religion" to believe?
Which moral code to look to and follow day by day,
How can we be positive we're on the *truthful* way?

The secular opinion on which deity to dote
Says "Whatever god can fit your mould. The one that floats your boat!
Don't worry if their theories or teachings don't ring true,
Just pick what suits your lifestyle best and fits in well with you."

I've heard it said "I know what's right, my views will never budge.
I want a god who just agrees and one who doesn't judge.
A god who doesn't challenge me, where *I* can be High Priest.
The one demanding zero change and strikes my conscience least."

"A god that asks no questions as it sits upon my shelf.
Basically a god that's just an image of myself."
But if we're top authority and rule our own dominion
Then "right and wrong" are just reduced to merely our opinion.

This means that truth is relative, our morals make the call
But then if truth *is* relative it's not really truth at all.
If rules and moral absolutes are there for our forsaking
Then all that we'll be left with is a god of our own making.

Or maybe we've reduced Him to "A Power in the sky."
We'll give our list of "wants" but then don't wait for His reply.
He's there for times of trouble when we need a favour, say
But let me ask the question, would we treat a *friend* that way?

Or would we have it in reverse and know *we're* being used
If every time they knock the door our kindness is abused?
If days of woe and need are the *only* days they call
Then all we'll find is selfishness, no friendship there at all.

No, God is not a genie in a bottle to exhort.
If this is how we view Him then sadly we fall short.
He knows *us* all by name and exactly how we work,
He knows each tiny detail and every little quirk.

Like any *real* relationship He loves us fervently
And if we've yet to find God then He calls us earnestly.
He longs for us to know Him in a real and awesome way.
Behold, He stands and knocks on all the hearts who've gone astray!

If we observe the human race we needn't look for long
To see mankind is wicked and there's clearly something wrong.
The problem is we're sinful, we rebelled against our King!
There's no denying we need help for all the mess we're in.

With nations fighting nations, all we see is war.
The politicians don't know who to look to anymore!
We search for hope and answers in these troubled times we live in,
Our hearts desire purpose for the days that we've been given.

For guidance on our future we must focus on the past,
It was Jesus Christ who warned us these things would come to pass.
So let's look back at Hist'ry, *who* did Jesus claim to be?
He said "To gain eternal life, all must follow *Me*."

His words professed divinity, He said He was God's Son.
He claimed to be the doorway to the life that is to come.
We're told it's "narrow-minded" to declare there's just "One Way"
But this is why we have to look at what the records say.

Though others claimed divinity, a fact none can refute,
The biggest difference of them all, they have no substitute!
There's only *One* who dealt with sin and *One* name that can save;
The God who took our punishment and left an empty grave!

The One and only living God, Jesus Christ Himself.
The God who made the sun and moon won't sit on any shelf!
For Jesus looked upon the Earth and saw the heartache there,
The King who left His Throne and came to save us from despair.

The One who gave up everything, who didn't close His eyes
To all the man-made hurt and pain, the God who heard our cries.
The One who had the power and the love within His heart
To face the Cross and see it through though *He* was torn apart.

The broken, bloodied, beaten form forsaken on the Tree;
The Man who died to give *us* life, now THAT'S the God for me!
And yet we still reject Him with the views we preconceive.
We close our minds to fact and truth and simply *won't* believe.

But even *if* we say that we do not believe in God,
The atheist's religion is the path that will be trod.
Some say, "You cannot prove your God, I won't rely on faith!"
But neither can you *disprove* Him and *disbelief* takes faith.

Whatever our hypothesis of how we came to be,
It all requires *faith* in things beyond what we can see
For none of us were there when first it all began.
We didn't see the dawn of time or start the age of man.

It really begs the question, how did life on Earth begin?
Who gave the Earth it's axis and direction of it's spin?
A singular explosion thirteen billion years ago?
A random act of *chaos* formed our *order* down below?

But even if we hold to this, it doesn't help explain
Where spatial matter came from so we'll seek the truth in vain.
For nothing comes from nothing, the errors here are rife
And even *science* says that life can only come from life!

We're told it's "Faith *or* Science" when there's really no dilemma,
Real science is to seek the truth not further an agenda.
To claim it proves God's "absence" is to really act the traitor,
Holding **faith** in **human logic** *over* **faith** in our **Creator**.

For Earth itself cries out of it's intelligent design!
We do not have to dig to find an influence Divine.
Scientific findings and the Bible coincide!
When both are founded in the truth the answers don't collide.

For science is a gift from God to further human knowledge.
"The Lab" should never contradict what's taught in Bible college
For all the Earth bears witness to a great and awesome Maker.
Creation says quite clearly that there *must* be a *Creator*!

But this is not so popular within the thoughts of man.
It means that we're **accountable**, of this we're not a fan.
We like to think *we're* in control and top the leader chart.
"*I* hold the reins and rule my life! *I'm* sovereign in my heart!"

We won't even consider that our actions might be judged.
We won't have morals scrutinised or reputations smudged!
We want to claim sole ownership and rights to our life story,
Rejecting rather fiercely we're created for *God's* glory.

The truth of our creation has all but been dissolved,
Instead we've all been brainwashed to believe mankind "evolved!"
For "Darwin's Evolution" isn't fact, it's just a thought!
We can't observe or test his claims and yet it's widely taught.

To base our lives around this lie would simply be naïve,
Without a shred of evidence we have to just "believe."
This tale of utter fiction leaves our spirits destitute;
Religion based on monkeys is a godless substitute.

I find it quite insulting and it gets me so irate
When humankind is just reduced to merely a primate!
My views on man's creation mean I'm called a "Bible junkie"
But I'd rather hold *God's* image than the image of a monkey!

How utterly undignified and really quite absurd!
This goes *against* true science and contradicts God's Word.
Mankind belongs to Jesus Christ and not within a zoo.
Why is this so challenging for man to submit to?

We cannot hang our disbelief on "lack of evidence."
It's not because we're "more evolved" with "high intelligence!"
You might have PHD's and boast the highest known I.Q
But all of this falls flat for *God* is cleverer than you.

It's really not a question of how many books we've read
For Socrates and Plato cannot help us when we're dead.
Faith in God is not reserved for those we view as weak.
Our *need* for God is not erased when on a "winning streak!"

It doesn't say "For God so loved the ugly, poor and dim."
The rich and the intelligent are also dead in sin!
The Bible says "For God so loved the *world* He gave His Son."
The sacrifice of Christ was on behalf of *everyone!*

Accepting this as truth is not to do with our brain tissue.
Denying that there *is* a God is really a heart issue
For what it all comes down to, no matter what we say,
We do not want to answer to a righteous God one day.

The thought of this infuriates and many shake their fist!
But deciding we believe in God does not *make* God exist!
He sits and reigns upon His Throne each day we live and breathe
Regardless what we think of Him or what we might believe!

Relinquishing our rule on life we have to lift our eyes,
Acknowledge with humility that God alone is wise.
He doesn't ask we leave our brains and reasoning at the door
But rather open up our minds to things dismissed before.

God didn't owe us *anything* for *we* rejected *Him*!
He would have been within His rights to leave us in our sin!
So no matter what philosophies or theorems we discuss
We only come to call on God because *He* first calls *us.*

To think we can erase Him with our disbelief or view
Is really catastrophic and a tragic thing to do.
There *is* a God in Heaven, Jesus Christ the King of kings
And whether we accept or not, this *is* the truth of things.

I won't sugar-coat the Gospel to appeal to "modern times."
This does not bring redemption or eradicate our crimes.
With souls at stake we must consider on a sober level,
If we don't submit to God then we're submitting to the devil.

I know at this some laugh and scoff and even get annoyed
But Satan *hates* the Cross because it's where he was destroyed!
He'll tolerate "religion" for that cannot touch his throne
But *dare* to preach the Gospel and his power's overthrown!

Let me ask the question, what's the name in vain we take?
You won't hear someone shout in pain, "Oh for Buddha's sake!"
It's only *Jesus'* name we use in order to blaspheme.
It's *His* name that offends us for it's *His* name that redeems!

It's *here* we find salvation which the devil knows too well.
Belittling the name of Christ, a tactic straight from Hell.
Our curses fall on *Jesus,* He's where warfare clearly lies
And yet we still deny the God who's right before our eyes!

But would we bet our life on it, there's no God in control?
Can we take the chance we *might* be wrong and gamble with our soul?
So let's just say there is no God and Heaven's just a taunt,
Is oblivion and emptiness *really* what we want?

Everything we are and every*thing* that we've achieved
Should *all* cease to exist and that's what we'd *choose* to believe?
The years that we spent learning should all be put to waste,
The *point* of our existence we just throw away with haste?

Our life has no real purpose, just a "cosmic accident."
It's ours to do with as we please, of *this* we're adamant.
No hope for life eternal, we'd just rather press "Delete."
Does that *really* satisfy the soul and make us feel complete?

Some say this life is all we've got, just make the most of things
But what about the countless lives where pain is all it brings?
"No God" will mean no justice with no hope to see them through.
All children born in war, tough luck for them but fine for you?

A hopeless, heartless message spoken only by the richest.
I guess with evolution it's "survival of the fittest!"
Why would we show kindness, telling others that we care?
Why would we be selfless and show willingness to share?

For if we're only animals then this is rather odd.
To claim that it's *humanity*, now *that* leads back to God.
He's the One who we reflect, this sets mankind apart.
It's *God* who puts compassion for another in our heart.

But even *if* we're "nice" there's still the issue of our sin.
God looks upon our *hearts* and we're all blackened from within.
I know this is a message that we do not want to hear,
An insult to our pride and a red flag to our fear.

We say it is our right that we decide who fits the bill
And this is true, I'd say it's what the Bible calls free-will!
God doesn't want a robot that's been programmed with no choice.
A mindless, thoughtless servant will not make our God rejoice.

Our praise is only genuine through hearts of adoration
For the Saviour of our souls and the God of all creation!
The free-will God has given will condemn or set us free
For Jesus said "I *Am* the Way" and "All must come to Me."

There is no padded fence with God so let's consider well;
Oblivion is not a choice. It's Heaven or it's Hell.
All roads in life *do* lead to God, it's certain that one day
We'll *all* come face to face with Him but then what will we say?

"I qualify for Heaven and think I pass the test
Because I went to Church one week and wore my Sunday best!"
"I qualify for Heaven for I lived as best I could.
I'd give myself nine out of ten for marks at being good!"

"I qualify for Heaven for I'm right in my own eyes.
I've earned my place up there and none can tell me otherwise!
He'll overlook my short-comings and focus on my traits.
And if God's so forgiving He should open up those Gates!"

But clever skills debating won't convince a Holy King
Who watched our every movement and saw our every sin.
When *my* turn comes before God's Throne there's one thing I can say,
"I qualify for Heaven for Jesus took my sins away!"

I qualify for Heaven from no merit of my own.
To get what I deserved, to deepest depths I would be thrown!
For all of us have fallen short, God's standard is *perfection*
And this is why we need to look to Jesus' Resurrection!

But the Cross offends so many and is often thrown aside.
It's the status equaliser and the leveller of pride
For Jesus had no favourites when He died upon that Tree.
There's no area in Heaven cordoned off marked "V.I.P."

God doesn't look at people in the way that *people* do.
Our status, creed and wealth can mean a lot to me and you.
He's not impressed by bank accounts if they be big or small;
He cares for our *eternity* so died to save us all.

Yes Jesus Christ loves everyone and paid the price of sin
For every Nationality and every shade of skin.
Examining the sinner's heart He looks beyond the face.
We're all created equal and we're all His human race.

He built the road to Heaven and His death paid every toll
And if we try to claim "no guilt" we're lying to our soul!
We must wrestle with our conscience! Dig deep and make a start!
We'll find we have a God shaped hole engraved within our heart!

Our life is like a jigsaw that has been left incomplete,
The picture finished off by Christ and naught else can compete!
Created by our Maker with this emptiness within
To make us search to *find* our God and fill that void with Him!

Nothing else will fit there, no pay cheque, job or house.
No hobby, clothes or passion, nor love from friend or spouse.
To live without our God will mean our soul will always thirst.
Let's trust our lives to Him and love the God who loved us first!

Don't settle for the devil's lies or say we'll "change things later."
Let's live the life Christ *bought* for us and live it with our Saviour.
Please don't deny your soul this peace and joy while you're still living
And know that when death's moment comes, the journey's
just beginning!

Be rich towards the Lord for in a few years we'll be gone
But when we know our King, in realms of Heaven we'll live on!
With hearts of gratitude we'll walk those golden streets one day
And praise God for eternity that Jesus built One Way.

SCRIPTURE REFERENCES

Jeremiah 9:23-24; Isaiah 43:10-11; Jeremiah 10:11; Acts 4:12;
1 John 5:12

READY ME

As I sat reading my daily devotional on the first day of 2012 the author of that particular day's excerpt asked me a question. He asked whether I had considered the thought that perhaps it might be this year that Jesus returns to claim His Bride. He then went on to ask, if I knew for a fact that it would be this year would it change the way I live my life in any way? Would it change the people I speak to and what I speak to them about? If I knew the days were running out when I would have an opportunity to share the Gospel would it change my priorities in any way?

I personally cannot wait for Jesus to call us home which I know could happen at any moment. I think if I'm honest though, I've found myself guilty of sometimes getting caught up in life and living as if His return is unlikely to happen today and more likely to be a future event. The danger of living with this attitude however is that it can lead to apathy and quench the desire to live full-out for Christ each day.

When I consider the fact that we don't know the day or the hour of Christ's return I think it brings an incentive to "keep on our toes" and to be watchful. It certainly helps to remind me that I need to utilise every opportunity He gives me to witness for Him because in reality, I never know when it'll be my last chance! His return might not be this year but then again it might be. It made me aware that I need to live with a strong awareness of the imminency of Christ's return as subsequently this will affect how fervently I share the Gospel with the people God brings into my life.

As Matthew 24:43-44 says,

> *"But know this, that if the master of the house had known what hour the thief would come, he would have watched and not*

allowed his house to be broken into. Therefore you also be ready, for the Son of Man is coming at an hour you do not expect."

I wanted to write a poem that would help remind me to keep my focus on Jesus and inspire me to live in such a way that I try to do the best I can with the time and resources God has given me. The time remaining is precious and rather than take the easier option of going into autopilot, I need to seek God's will on a daily basis and prepare for His return.

Quite a tough challenge with all the distractions the world has to offer but that's why for me it's a daily reminder so that when the day comes when the trumpet sounds and Jesus does come back to claim His Bride, I can hopefully say with confidence, "Lord, I'm ready."

POEM

Ready me for Your return, ready me I pray.
I yearn for our reunion on that great and awesome day.
Fill me with a passion fierce, anoint my soul anew.
Rivet my attention on becoming more like You.

Ready me to share my hope at any given time
And give a reason for my faith with confidence divine.
Focus all my energies on serving You my King,
On guiding countless souls to the protection of Your wing.

Fill me with the strength to live a holy life so pure
So others then may realise my hope in You is sure.
Please help them see my faith is not an empty desperation,
It's not a wistful, fleeting hope but solid expectation.

Ready me to fight the fight and run a worthy race
So I am not ashamed when You and I come face to face!
Give me strength to point the lost to where each soul finds rest,
Regardless of the outcome let me always try my best.

Keep me from distractions that would pull Your plans aside
For I know not the time at which You'll come to claim Your bride.
At any moment it could be the last chance that I'll get
To share the Gospel's truth with those who do not know You yet.

So if lethargy overtakes or fearful thoughts of doubt,
Please give a quick reminder that our time is running out.
Behold, You're coming quickly! Could it be within the year?
Help me keep this sober thought with reverential fear.

Let it be the driving force to live each day for You,
To set a good example Lord in all I say and do.
For if I think of Your return, it changes my perspective,
I focus more on others' needs than matters introspective.

My thoughts can fall so easily to cares and woes internal.
Please lift my eyes from troubles small to those of the eternal.
For life on Earth is temporal and each soul must decide
Where they will spend eternity, where forever they'll abide.

Ready me to share this truth with love, without condition.
To spread the news of Jesus' grace must be my greatest mission!
Lord fill me with compassion, with a heart to reach the lost,
Let Jesus Christ be on my lips no matter of the cost.

So as I watch for Your return, a truth not taken lightly,
Lord let my waist be girded and my lamps be burning brightly.
I long for You to claim Your Bride, Your face at last I'll see.
As I await that awesome day, dear Lord please ready me.

SCRIPTURE REFERENCES

Luke 12:35-40

VALENTINE'S DAY

INSPIRATION

I have to thank several FaceBook statuses on Valentine's Day 2012 for my inspiration for the first few verses of this poem. I was truly fascinated as I witnessed the different reactions to this man-made day, a day when romance and confessions of love apparently must rush into our lives! It seems that this has the potential to really affect our emotions and self esteem depending on where we feel we stand with our "love-life" status!

The stimulus was the same but the reactions were varied. I witnessed certain couples exuberantly gush about their Valentine's Day plans and gifts to the envy of everyone else on FaceBook. In contrast I noticed many singletons either drew attention to their status by cracking a self deprecating joke or else posted a heart-broken message that suggested they would be wallowing in self-pity all evening. It seemed that some people felt unable to face the apparent "humiliation" of being single on Valentine's Day! What pressure this day brings!

It got me thinking about our need and desire for love in life. Of course the "Valentine's Day love" focuses on romantic love between two people but ultimately it boils down to the same thing; the vast majority of us desire to have love and acceptance in our lives.

I started to consider how the love of other people certainly has it's place and importance in life but there is no greater and more important love than the love from God and knowing that in His eyes we are accepted. To know Jesus and feel loved and accepted by Him makes everything else pale by comparison because through Him we can learn what true, unconditional love is like in it's purest form. I say this with confidence because we know from the Bible that "God is love."

As 1 Corinthians 13:4-8 says,

"Love suffers long and is kind; love does not envy; love does not parade itself, is not puffed up; does not behave rudely, does not seek it's own, is not provoked, thinks no evil; does not rejoice in iniquity, but rejoices in the truth; bears all things, believes all things, hopes all things, endures all things. Love never fails."

Really, this is a wonderful description of God! I wanted to write a poem that draws attention towards the true source of love, Jesus Christ and how when we've got Him in our hearts it doesn't matter if we're single, dating, engaged or married. We can always feel loved, accepted and treasured beyond belief with Jesus, not just in this life but also in the next.

POEM

"Roses are red and violets are blue."
They come with a card, "Love from me to you."
The flowers and chocolates are out on display.
The message is clear, it's Valentine's Day!

The day of the year we're encouraged to show
Our feelings of love and romance for our beau.
Or say in a letter how love-struck you are
To one whom you secretly like from afar.

Let feelings be known before it's too late
And pluck up the courage to ask for a date!
The hope that the postman will put out his back
Bringing you letters of love in his sack!

For some it's a day when they're filled with a dread
As every shop window displays gifts of red.
Love hearts and roses and cupids with wings,
With thoughts of love lost it can pull the heart strings.

Now some who are single feel bound to their house,
Avoiding the ones off to dine with their spouse.
They feel like the loneliest soul on the Earth
As if numbers of cards reveals how much they're worth!

If the room isn't filled with "Valentine's stuff"
The poor person feels like they're not good enough!
"Nobody loves me!" I've heard people say.
"I wish I could just hibernate for the day!"

"With couples out dining I'll be on my own.
The *shame* of this day when it's spent all alone!"
There's pressure to be "coupled-up" it would seem
And Valentine's really can knock self-esteem.

I notice a woman with nothing to hide,
She carries a ribboned bouquet with such pride!
It seems it's a statement for all to see,
"I'm special to someone who cares about me."

Though Valentine's Day can bring many much joy,
It also can niggle and start to annoy.
Couples who try to convince and persuade
Their partnership must be the best ever made!

Extravagant gifts are "a sign of their love"
And their lives fit together like hand fits in glove.
They want you to witness their public display
And then you find out they broke up the next day!

Though I do not begrudge showing *real* gratitude
For genuine signs of affection are good
But fanciful shows so overtly displayed,
I can't help but feel it's a little "man-made."

So whether this day makes your heart ache or sing,
It seems pretty clear we all want the same thing.
Whoever we are there's a thought we admire,
To have love in our life is our greatest desire.

We strive to attain it whatever the cost
But we won't know *real* love 'til we look to the Cross.
The Cross where Christ Jesus paid for our sin,
He cleared every debt though He owed not a thing.

Though many have heard of the Cross, times before
It's become just a sign for "religion," no more.
Or an image of fashion to wear on a chain
But I ask you to look to the Cross once again.

For there lies a pivotal moment in time,
It's affect so profound and it's purpose divine.
The statement is clear, the meaning is true,
You're special to *Jesus* who cares about you.

Sent by the Father, a bridge He'd to build.
Christ died in our place so this task He fulfilled.
Determined God's love for mankind would prevail,
Now the proof of this love is the scar from each nail.

If *you* want to feel like you're precious and dear
Then call out to Jesus and He will draw near.
Married or single, somewhere in-between,
You'll treasure Christ's love as the greatest you've seen.

Now I know human love and the joy it can bring
But nothing compares to the love of our King.
For His will not tire nor ever run dry,
He never will leave you nor bid you goodbye.

You're *His* work of art! A thought to embrace.
A special "one-off" who can't be replaced!
A cherished companion, you're God's number one
And *His* love holds promise for the life that's to come.

Our Strength, our Provider, our Counsellor too,
The One who created each fibre of you.
Our faithful Companion who gives our souls rest,
Whose plan for our life is always what's best.

Our Guide, our Protector, our wonderful Friend
Who's promised He's with us, right to the end.
With Christ in our hearts we have nothing to fear,
For God shows *His* love EVERY day of the year!

Just look to the Cross where His blood was shed,
You'll see your salvation was *His* gift in red.
So on Valentine's Day it is good to recall,
Christ's story of love is the greatest of all.

This Valentine's may be your best or your worst,
But always remember that Christ loved you first.
The gift of our Saviour is reason to say
EVERY day of the year, Happy Valentine's Day!

SCRIPTURE REFERENCES

1 John 4: 9-19

AFTERWORD

A lady once came to me when I was visiting a Church and told me that this poem held a special place in her heart. She had recently lost her father but she shared with me that while he was in hospital over Valentine's Day she had read this poem to him.

He wasn't a believer at that point but said that hearing about God's love had really moved him. Thanks to this wonderful lady's prayers and her faithful witness to her father, he gave his heart to Jesus before he passed away. I couldn't help but praise God for His faithfulness at hearing this wonderful story of redemption! Thanks to Jesus I'm looking forward to meeting this dear man when I get to Heaven.

THE BEGINNING OF SORROWS

It seems that the more time passes the further away from God society is moving. Sometimes when I look at the lost condition of the world and hear how hateful people can be towards God it fills my heart with despair. I often think of the Bible passage from Romans 1:28-32 which reads,

"And even as they did not like to retain God in their knowledge, God gave them over to a debased mind, to do those things which are not fitting; being filled with all unrighteousness, sexual immorality, wickedness, covetousness, maliciousness; full of envy, murder, strife, deceit, evil-mindedness; they are whisperers, backbiters, haters of God, violent, proud, boasters, inventors of evil things, disobedient to parents, undiscerning, untrustworthy, unloving, unforgiving, unmerciful; who, knowing the righteous judgment of God, that those who practice such things are deserving of death, not only do the same but also approve of those who practice them."

It's clear to see that the world is rapidly going in the direction that the Bible said it would. If it hadn't been for God's foreknowledge of this and His promise that this would be a sign of His imminent return, I think the despair would be too much to handle. Knowing that Jesus is in control no matter how godless the world becomes is a huge comfort and encouragement to me and these feelings inspired my poem "The Beginning Of Sorrows."

POEM

O' soul of mine do not be vexed by troubles in this life complexed.
I see man's hateful views of God while depravation gains applaud.
At blasphemies do not be shocked and know that God will not
be mocked.
To curse Him is a grave mistake for vengeance is the Lord's to take.

O' inner calm do not retreat, these evil days are bitter sweet
For God has said that these are signs of Christ's return, the end
of times.
So heart of mine be troubled not, God said "As in the days of Lot."
These times are dark with wicked ways, polluted by debauched displays.

Denying proof of God's creation, believing we're a chimp's relation!
Preferring to associate with *monkeys* than the God we hate!
We'd rather choose a mammal's story than honour God and give
Him glory.
Though hearts embrace these lies absurd, stay true to Christ and preach
the Word.

Be bold and represent the Light, bring rays of hope to pierce the night!
For there are those who wield the sword and say they kill to "praise
their Lord."
In spite of what their acts proclaim they'll waken to eternal shame
So let me focus not on strife but on the God who brings us *life*!

O' peace of mine return to me. I once was blind but now I see!
Now Heaven will receive my soul so rest and know God's in control
For He's the Author of all life and will return to end this strife.
So use this time to pray for those who do not share the Saviour's robes.

These troubled times my soul can face with Christ who'll help me run
the race.
The devil's plans my Lord will quell and give me strength to finish well.
So hands of mine pick up your Sword and keep your focus on the Lord!
Pray make my life a Christ-like story. Let me live for Jesus' glory!

SCRIPTURE REFERENCES

Matthew 24:3-8

THANK YOU MUM

INSPIRATION

I wrote this poem because I wanted to show my gratitude to my Mum for everything she's done for me over the years. From the little things such as putting plasters on my knees and comforting me when I fell to the much bigger things in life. Things such as her wisdom, guidance, encouragement and teaching me about the truth of the Gospel of Jesus Christ.

In hindsight I can really see the constant, godly influence my Mum has been in my life and how she has stayed faithful to her ministry even when I wasn't staying faithful to mine. Although this poem has been written by me for my Mum personally, my hope is that others may be able to relate to the sentiment, the emotions and the gratitude of the poem too.

My main desire is that it can be an encouragement to anyone who has been called to be a parent, not just mothers but fathers as well. I hope it can inspire and encourage parents to bring Jesus into their relationship with their children. As I look back at my life and see how my Mum has done that with me, it really brings to mind Isaiah 55:11 where the Lord says,

"So shall My word be that goes forth from My mouth; it shall not return to Me void, But it shall accomplish what I please, and it shall prosper in the thing for which I sent it."

I can really see how the truth of this verse has worked through my life as there were years when I didn't want to know about God or hear about Jesus but the seeds that had already been planted were never uprooted. God's Word never left me and my Mum always stayed faithful in her witness to me through her words, actions and attitude towards things.

The very fact that I'm in a place spiritually where I can write a poem like this is a testament to my Mum's godly influence and I'll be eternally grateful for her continual love and prayers. For too many reasons to list, this poem is called "Thank You Mum."

POEM

Another "Mother's Day" is here and it's the perfect time
To send you gifts and buy you pretty flowers in their prime!
Although I know my card and gifts will brighten up your day,
They cannot quite express to you the things I'd like to say.

I'd like to take this time to share some things I'm thankful for,
You haven't been just "Mum" to me, you've also been much more.
To think of every memory and all that we've been through,
Please hear and know I'm grateful Mum and want to say "Thank you."

Thank you for your selflessness, the patience you have shown,
For all the times you put me first, the love that you've made known.
For every tear you wiped, for every plaster on my knee,
For every hug and cuddle that you gave so earnestly.

Encouraging my interests, you guided me in ways
That helped me to develop gifts I'd use throughout my days.
Pursue my passions fervently, your wisdom showed me how.
I know without your help I wouldn't be where I am now.

Thank you for my sister, she's a blessing from above.
Thanks to you and Dad I have a lifetime with her love.
We journey life together through the laughter and the tears,
We share each happy moment as we grow throughout the years.

She isn't just my sister though, she's also my best friend
And thanks to faith in Christ I know our love will never end.
We also have eternity to share our special bond.
My gratitude for her is without measure, far beyond.

Thanks for introducing me to the Saviour of the Earth,
For showing me the One who gave me life and second birth.
For pointing me toward the Cross where Jesus died for me,
For showing me the only way my soul could be set free.

Thank you for your years of prayer, for never giving in.
Thank you for your faith Mum and for pointing me to Him.
I'm grateful that you taught me of the way that's right and true.
I only pray that one day I'm a mum as good as you.

I know you'll squirm and shift for compliments are hard to hear
But even when the times get tough, you always persevere.
I grew up in a home with Mother's care that has sufficed.
You've loved me unconditionally. In this you mirror Christ.

You share in all my problems for you're there to lend an ear.
The times we talk and chat I always cherish and hold dear.
I'm always free to be myself, I never feel suppressed.
I clearly see with you Mum I have been so truly blessed.

I'm sure I've pushed and tried you but within the role of "Mum,"
I know that I can safely say this *is* a job well done!
Your life has been a blessing to so many all around,
A Mother and a friend like you are very rarely found.

So Mum, I hope you know how much I cherish you so dear,
Not just on "Mother's Day" but *every* day throughout the year!
I treasure you with all my heart, I'm grateful through and through
And thank my Saviour every day for blessing me with you.

SCRIPTURE REFERENCES

Proverbs 31:30-31; Proverbs 22:6

The Devil's Workshop

We know that as God's children the devil can't steal our salvation. He can never rob us of what Jesus paid for with His blood on the Cross. As my Pastor says, "You can't have eternal life temporarily!"

Satan can however try to rob us of many other things in our lives. Things such as our joy, peace, good relationships with other people and the power of our testimony. Nothing ruins our witness quicker than hypocrisy or a compromised lifestyle. The Bible tells us in 1 Peter 5:8,

"Be sober, be vigilant; because your adversary the devil walks about like a roaring lion, seeking whom he may devour."

The tools Satan uses will only ever seek to destroy and tear down what God has created and my poem "The Devil's Workshop" addresses this subject. I began to write it as I was thinking with sadness one day about how there are so many different ways the devil can accomplish his wicked purposes and so often it's through people. Even Christians can be used to hurt others if they're not careful and this is because the devil's devices are very subtle but extremely effective and completely destructive. It made me realise how important it is for us to not be "ignorant of his devices" lest Satan should take advantage of us. (2 Corinthians 2:11)

These were the thoughts that first inspired me to start writing my poem. As I continued to write I found that the words began to address the reality of spiritual warfare on a much deeper level and subsequently the importance of staying rooted and grounded in Jesus Christ.

My hope is that this poem can be an encouragement to all Christians to stand fast in our faith and to trust God no matter how the battle rages, always remembering the words of 1 John 4:4,

"He who is in you is greater than he who is in the world."

POEM

O' wretched tools in Satan's keep, a deadly whirlwind you will reap!
A vast array for him to use. So many different tools to choose
And not to build or to create but to destroy and devastate.
To wreck, to ravage and to break. To cause much sorrow and heartache.

A grand selection there to try, some lying lips, a jealous eye
To separate the closest brothers and envy blessings poured on others.
A bitter heart to poison you and also saw your peace in two.
A temper hot that's roused with ease, a tool to use just as he please.

A fiery tongue with flames of red, the sharpest tool in Satan's shed
For words cut deep just like a knife and hurt those dearest in your life.
An angry soul that knows no rest will put each loved one to the test;
With daily pain they try to manage a backlog of the years of damage.

A wrench of steel that twists the truth and lies that disregard
God's proof.
He toils with his darkest magic and chisels at society's fabric.
Instilling hearts with lusts abnormal, convincing man
perversion's normal.
To do what's pleasing in our sight, that right is wrong and wrong
is right.

Or entertain a selfish heart and dearest friends are ripped apart.
With words of gossip cruelly spoken, loyalty and trust is broken.
If unrepentant hearts are there the damage goes beyond repair.
Then holiness that's been displayed is nothing but a masquerade.

Refusing Godly admonition, seeking only vain ambition
For when great works of God are done some must be seen as
"Number One!"
But what's behind the words we speak? *Whose* glory is it that we seek?
For pride will only serve itself, another tool from Satan's shelf.

Within his shed what's this I see? Some tools are specialised for me!
O' God forbid that I succumb to work done by the evil one!
But it may not be done by choice so I must seek my Master's voice
Or discontentment in my life will steal my joy and stir up strife.

For Satan only need observe where I am weak and lose my nerve
For him to know what tool is best to use on me to gain success.
An angry word or quick reply can raise the heat and sparks will fly!
Or if I won't admit I'm wrong then pride prevails, my witness gone.

Distraction is a mighty tool, his scheming I must overrule!
His meddling and vile intention often strives for my attention.
Anything to keep my eyes from Scriptures that will make me wise
For when I draw my Bible near it strikes him cold with dread and fear!

He'll make me feel like I am worthless and my life is lacking purpose
To shift my focus from above, to make me doubt and lose my love
But Satan is the master liar, this plan is just to steal my fire.
Discouragement must not take root! With Christ my life *can* bear
good fruit.

It's *vital* that I recognise the warfare that's before my eyes.
With flesh and blood I do not wrestle though failure dwells within
this vessel.
I war with powers straight from hell that know my weaknesses too well.
I would despair and try to flee if victory were up to me!

Against his might I don't compare until I open up in prayer.
This battle won't be fought alone, I'll seek my strength from
Jesus' Throne
For when I call upon God's name His armour will protect my frame.
Though I alone may cause no fear, I say *His* name and God draws near!

In terror I will not retreat, I'll wear His armour to defeat
The plans and schemes and fiery darts that Satan pitches at my heart.
My shield of faith will quench the flame as I stand fast in Jesus' name!
Though tests will come I'll lift my sword and fight with strength from
Christ my Lord.

Whatever battles come my way I will withstand the evil day!
Though I may face the world's reproof I'll gird my waist with
Jesus' truth
And with the helmet of salvation I'll watch and pray with supplication
For many live in fear and doubt and time is quickly running out.

For Satan and his minions know they face the fiery depths below.
At Jesus' name they try to flee for none has greater strength than He!
But evil *can't* escape His sight and who can stand against *His* might?
Their wicked reign my God will quell and chain them to the pits
of hell.

Start running Satan! Run from me! My Saviour stands between you
and me!
And though you curse my life with pain I *still* will worship Jesus' name!
You are no match for Christ the King and you know well you
cannot win!
Your tools won't stand against my sword, the double sided Word
of God!

The *power* there that knows no age, the truth to find on every page!
It tells me Jesus loves me dear and all my life He'll hold me near.
It tells me that my debt and sin were paid in full by Christ my King!
What blessèd news for every nation, Jesus Christ is our Salvation!

Dearest brethren fear no harm, let *God's* strength lift your fighting arm!
Our faith is where success is made and what are tools against a *blade*?
Wield the Sword and dare expose the truth of Jesus Christ to those
Still in bondage, trapped in sin! Guide the lost towards their King!

Knowing as the truth embeds that this is what the devil dreads
For in their sin he'd watch them drown so tear the devil's
strongholds down!
Share the Gospel! Use the Word! To hide this Light would be absurd!
The Light of God he cannot manage and we can do a lot of damage.

So turn the tables! Make *him* flee! Refuse to simply bow the knee
To anything from Satan's throne; we serve our God and God alone!
Let Satan wear his self-made crown, he *knows* his kingdom's
coming down!
So wretched tools in Satan's keep, go back into your den so deep.

In God's protection we'll abide, we *know* we're on the winning side!
We'll preach the Word, redeem the time and as we wait the final sign
We'll stand together strong and firm and run this race 'til
Christ's return.
In victory our hearts will soar for Jesus Christ has won this war!

SCRIPTURE REFERENCES

Ephesians 6:10-20

THE TEA TEST

One day I was chatting to a Christian acquaintance of mine when he mentioned how his wife felt quite strongly about the subject of "appropriate attire" for Christians. As I walked home later that day I started to think about my own journey in this slightly grey area. At this point in time I had been walking with the Lord for six years and I started to think about how Jesus had really worked in my heart regarding this topic. I know for many people the issue of appearance really isn't a big deal but for me it was something I felt I really needed to examine in those early months of my Christian walk.

To put things into context, when I gave my heart to Jesus I was a youthful twenty four year old woman living in London, performing in the West End show "Chicago" and therefore was immersed in the image conscious world of Performing Arts. Taking into consideration that your image can very much influence how successful you are in this profession and can sometimes even dictate whether you get the job or not, you could say I had an invested interested in how I presented myself to the world. I wouldn't say it consumed me but it was rather high up on my priority list and what I wore could at times be influenced by quite a worldly perspective.

When I dedicated my life to Jesus however one of the first things I questioned was "what would be 'appropriate' to wear as a Christian?" As a "baby" in the Lord, I was just beginning to discover my new identity in Christ. Subsequently I found myself going through a time of wondering whether being a Christian meant I had to stop dressing the way I wanted to and instead have to start wearing dowdy, shapeless clothes that would be deemed more "appropriate." Thankfully the Holy Spirit stepped in and proved to be a wonderful Teacher on how to glorify God through self expression!

Looking back, it was a gradual process and it had nothing to do with legalism. No one was telling me "you can or can't wear this" or "you should or shouldn't look like that." It was because I now found that I wanted to make sure I was dressed appropriately for my God and the only voice speaking to me on this subject was the voice of the Holy Spirit. I felt that if my image was screaming the message "look at me!" then how could I ask people to focus on the far more important message of "look at Jesus?" The two didn't seem to go together to me but neither did I find the thought of spending the rest of my life in frumpy, plain clothing particularly appealing!

What you see of the "outer person" is very often a reflection of what's going on with the "inner person" so I wanted to make sure these two areas were sending the same signals so that I'd be able to tell people about Jesus without feeling like a hypocrite. My desire was to find a happy medium where I still felt that I could keep individuality and youth in my appearance but without compromising myself as a Christian and as someone who professes godliness.

As I've grown in the Lord over the years I've found that my desires and areas of focus have changed greatly. Don't get me wrong, I still love the odd shopping spree but I certainly don't face the same dilemmas like I used to! When it comes to taking care of my appearance I feel much more settled and confident in who I am in Christ. This was not the case however in the first year of my Christian walk and it was something that I felt I needed to address if I was going to be an effective witness for Jesus.

For this reason I decided to write this poem in retrospect and from my early Christian point of view. My hope is that it may be able to encourage anyone else who may be going through a similar experience no matter how long they've been walking with the Lord or whether they're male or female. I don't think it's an issue that's gender specific or even necessarily just to do with clothing but rather it's an issue of expressing what's in our heart.

Through prayer and God's gentle teaching I found a way that allowed me to be at peace with God and also with my appearance. I'm not claiming to have an irrefutable technique that will work for everyone or even to being a particularly stylish dresser! It's just a light-hearted poem that describes a process that I went through. I wish to share the point of view that there can be joy and liberation in self expression and individuality as well as walking hand in hand with our Saviour. After all, our Creator doesn't stifle us and put us in a box, He gives us space to express our unique personalities, reveals to us who we really are and sets us free!

POEM

So Jesus is my Saviour now, my life belongs to Him.
I've opened up my heart and I've repented of my sin.
I'm glad I'm on this path and I accept the Bible's truth.
I'm grateful that He's found me while I still have years of youth!

Now every week to Church I go, I feel as light as air!
But then I start to wonder, "What's appropriate to wear?"
I've never questioned this before, I'd do just as I please
But something now is different and I don't feel quite at ease.

The tabloids say to "Strut my stuff" and "Flaunt what I've been given!"
But now I fear that this is not a godly way of living.
So now that I'm a Christian do I dress just like a nun?
Be donned in black from head to toe and ruin all the fun?

A common misconception which I've heard asked rather smugly,
"Don't Christians dress in dowdy clothes and aren't they always ugly?"
"A Christian's not allowed nice clothes, it's seen as too enticing!
You have to always look depressed or else you're too inviting."

A sweeping, worldly statement and so wrong in many ways!
If beauty only lies in clothes we live in troubled days!
But still, there *is* the interest to take care of one's appearance
And not feel like all clothes must come from sales entitled "Clearance!"

Why bless me with my freedom then to stifle me in black
And sentence me to life where all I wear is one big sack?
I can't say this appeals or sounds like something I should do.
These "rules" don't sound like anything that God would put
me through.

No, God created genders and He set us both apart,
He made us male and female and he put this in each heart.
I wish to honour God without inviting dullest tedium.
I give it up in prayer for there *must* be a happy medium!

I want to find a balance where I honour Jesus' name
But still appreciate His gifts, in this there is no shame!
And then there's my desire where I want to find a spouse.
I can't do that in clothes I'd only wear around the house!

But if a man is looking at the body parts I flaunt,
If *that's* what turns his head, is that the kind of man I want?
What happens when my skin grows old, my face looks less than fresh?
I'd rather he took interest in my *character* than flesh.

For if I want a marriage that's secure and everlasting,
I'd like a *deeper* love with an attraction longer lasting!
I put God first and know that I can find a way demure,
A woman seeking God *can* dress in stylish ways I'm sure!

And so with prayer I find how to decipher what is best.
I ask myself the question, does this outfit pass "The Tea Test?"
Please let me clarify and tell you and what I mean by this;
If I were meeting God for tea, would I turn up in *this*?

Would I feel at ease with God and perfectly composed
Or would I be ashamed at what my flashy outfit shows?
For if I start to shift and feel I have to rearrange
That's probably the perfect sign that I should go and change!

For if I'm out in public in a small, tight, skimpy thing
How can I then represent my righteous God and King?
If I said "I'm a Christian!" would a stranger be surprised?
For if my clothes don't match my talk I'd say I'm compromised.

If I can't share the Gospel due to unwise sense of dress
I may be out of line for one proclaiming godliness.
But if I know I'd meet with God and wear this comfortably
I know I'm fine for in real life Christ's *always* there with me!

He sees me every day and knows exactly what I wear!
He watches me put make-up on and how I style my hair.
A saying that I've heard before I'd like to now repeat it,
"If the barn door needs a lick of paint then go ahead and paint it!"

A little bit of care won't mean I'm catching every eye
But won't ask God to share me with whoever's walking by!
I'd rather wear my *love* for God for everyone to see
Than clothes for all occasions with the message "Look at me!"

I realise my body isn't mine to flaunt and show
For Jesus paid a price for me and now to Him I owe
Everything I have in life, He set me free from sin
And now my heart's *desire* is to praise and worship Him!

So when one comes to Christ and starts to question their dress sense
The "Frumpy/Flashy" battle is what often will commence!
But God has *liberated* us and as the fairer sex,
The case of "what to wear," it doesn't have to be complex.

I make the most of things without offending the vicinity.
I dress to honour God but without staunching femininity!
So what should be the dress code for the one God calls His daughter?
I think for me the rule will be, let's flatter it, not flaunter!

SCRIPTURE REFERENCES

Romans 12:1

AFTERWORD

I've had the pleasure of sharing this poem at a couple of women's groups and a young ladies conference. My hope is that this poem may really speak to the younger generation in particular or anyone who has been put under the weight of legalism from others. I pray it may be used by many to help people really discover the liberation Jesus brings to our lives as we seek to honour Him.

BE STILL

I wrote this poem during a very difficult time in my life and the words are what came from my heart as I sat in the late hours one night thinking about the stresses of the day. That evening I knew I had a choice. I could spend the night worrying about my future, stressing over the things that were happening to me that I had no control over and subsequently getting myself into a teary mess over it all or I could offer up my fears to the Lord as a sacrifice. I could ask Him to lift the burden of stress from me and replace it with His peace.

I discovered very quickly how faithful God is to His Word. I learned that if I'm willing to let go of negative things and put my trust in Him, He is faithful to take them from me and as Psalm 46:1 says,

"God is our refuge and strength, a very present help in trouble."

The truth of this verse spoke so powerfully into my life that night because my situation didn't change but God changed me within it. It was nothing less than a small miracle within my heart because all of a sudden I had that God-given peace that surpasses all understanding. By all accounts I could have sat there worrying all night about my circumstances but what good would it have done me? God tells us not to worry about our lives because He is in control and He loves us. As hard as it may be to believe in the middle of hardship, we know that God is working through all of our circumstances and for our benefit! As we read in Romans 8:28,

"And we know that all things work together for the good to those who love God, to those who are the called according to His purpose."

I really learned that night that no matter how the battles rage during the day and quite possibly will rage again the next, God can grant us peace and give our weary souls much needed rest if we seek Him. As Philippians 4:6-7 says,

"Be anxious for nothing, but in everything by prayer and supplication, with thanksgiving, let your requests be made known to God; and the peace of God, which surpasses all understanding, will guard your hearts and minds through Christ Jesus."

There is always refuge, comfort, strength, peace and encouragement to be found in Jesus Christ, even when our circumstances are screaming the opposite. What a wonderful privilege to know such a caring, loving, wise and powerful God.

POEM

Troubles of the day, depart and worry not my mind
For as I still my weary soul to seek my God I find
The woes that weigh my spirit down within the light of day
Are lifted by His mighty hands and gently fade away.

I meditate within my heart and sacrifice my fear
And as I lay my head to rest I feel my Saviour near.
Instead of fretful, sleepless nights where torments never cease,
I contradict my circumstance and slumber deep in peace.

Although I know when I awake I'll face these woes again,
I'll find my strength in Jesus Christ, my never failing Friend.
He keeps my mind from dwelling on the trials of tomorrow
For that won't help to heal me and will bring me extra sorrow.

For if I look through worldly eyes I cannot see a way,
With God *all* things are possible and so again I pray.
I'm comforted by Scripture and I know He's in control,
To read of Jesus' power puts such peace within my soul.

A peace I cannot understand but in it I'll abide.
Whatever comes my way I'll face with Jesus by my side.
I trust my Saviour's goodness and His sovereign plan for me;
His purposes are wise, the bigger picture He can see.

I'm reassured by Jesus as I feel the night draw in.
What privilege is mine to give my burdens all to Him.
So troubles of the day, depart. I'm safe within His will.
The dark of night envelopes me, so rest my soul. Be still.

Scripture References

Psalm 46:10; Psalm 4:8; 1 Peter 5:7

PSALM 23

INSPIRATION

I'm sure it'll come as no surprise that my inspiration for this poem came from Psalm 23! The passage reads,

"The Lord is my Shepherd; I shall not want. He makes me to lie down in green pastures; He leads me beside the still waters. He restores my soul; He leads me in the paths of righteousness for His name's sake. Yea, though I walk through the valley of the shadow of death, I will fear no evil; For You are with me; Your rod and Your staff, they comfort me. You prepare a table before me in the presence on mine enemies; You anoint my head with oil; My cup runs over. Surely goodness and mercy shall follow me all the days of my life; And I will dwell in the house of the Lord forever."

This Psalm has a very special place in my heart. The first time the Lord really spoke to me through this chapter was when I was questioning whether a particular job was going to be an honouring project for me to be involved in. I wanted to make sure I was putting God first and not my own ambition so when I brought this to Him in prayer the Holy Spirit led me to Psalm 23.

He spoke to me very clearly through these verses and put such a peace in my heart that the job in question was indeed God's plan for me, that He had prepared the path ahead and that it was for His name's sake that I would go there. It gave me such joy and security knowing that I could proceed with confidence and that I was in the centre of God's will by taking on this particular job.

About a year and a half later I was going through a really tough time with persecution in the workplace. A particular colleague wasn't happy to be working with a born-again Christian and was making this fact perfectly clear. As I was praying about this very unpleasant situation that had been dragging on for months, the Lord took me to Psalm 23 for a second time. I remembered the original promises He made before I had even started the job.

I was reminded that it was His will for me to be there, He would protect and guide me through any "valleys" and that it was for His glory that I was there at all. It filled me with a resolution to keep running the race and keep looking to Him for my strength and motivation.

It wasn't long after this second trip to Psalm 23 that the situation at work was brought to a head and dealt with in a godly manner. I witnessed God's faithfulness in an amazing way through this and just as He had promised I could see that He was with me. He comforted and protected me and I could certainly see God's goodness and mercy following me all the days of my life!

Having this history with Psalm 23, it was very interesting when I was led specifically to it for a third time and this time my situation was completely different again. The verses reminded me more than ever about how we can be in the centre of God's will even in the midst of a hardship. I recalled His faithfulness through the trials I had been through before and felt He was encouraging me not to despair about my situation now. Just like the times before, Jesus was with me, He was in control and would see me through it.

I'm incredibly grateful for the way the Lord has encouraged and blessed me through the few verses of Psalm 23. In my life it's proved to be a wonderful reminder of God's care, guidance, protection and faithfulness. With such wonderful inspiration to draw from I wrote the poem "Psalm 23."

POEM

Psalm 23, O' how I love thee. You fill my heart with delight.
The Lord uses thee to reassure me, reminding me of His might.
My thoughts of despair are culled and laid bare as I read of my
Shepherd and Lord.
Knowing He's in control brings peace to my soul and slays all my fear
like a sword.

I trust in His plan and I'm safe in His palm though I walk through the shadows of death.
Though I see not a thing I know Christ is my King and has been since my very first breath.
This life is not mine and God sees down the line, He knows what I can and can't take.
Though I face the unknown I know I'm not alone and will live life for Christ Jesus' sake.

In life I can see of how God has led me, I've journeyed to waters so still.
Though trials now come I follow the Son so trust and submit to His will.
Though I may shed a tear my soul will not fear, He knows what my days have in store.
The table's prepared and He's already there, He's been faithful to me times before.

Anointing my head, He's my daily bread though the outcome I can't know or tell.
Killing doubts that annoy for come sorrow or joy in the house of the Lord I will dwell.
He's prepared me a place so as I lift my face my cup runneth over, so blessed.
With His goodness and strength I can run any length, with His power I'll pass any test.

Wherever I go let my gratitude show though I don't understand all His ways.
His mercy and love will protect from above and will follow me all of my days.
Psalm 23, O' how I love thee. Your comfort is beyond compare.
The Lord uses thee to reassure me that I'm precious and safe in His care.

Scripture References

2 Corinthians 4:7-10

TOOTHPASTE ETIQUETTE

INSPIRATION

I've heard it said that when a man and a woman get married it can be like two rough stones being brought together and the more time they spend dwelling side by side the smoother they become. Having been married since 2009 which is a relatively short time in the grand scale of marriage, I have to say I can see the truth in this analogy. After all, marriage brings two flawed people together who then have to learn how to dwell peaceably with one another!

Some couples may find this easier than others but it's pretty much a guarantee that a difference in opinion or a conflict in method will arise over something at some point. This brings with it the decision to either continue in conflict or find a compromise. I've found that learning how to adapt seems to be vital for a good marriage and the more both parties are prepared to put the needs of the other first, the smoother things seem to go!

Of course the whole institute of marriage was created by God to reflect His relationship with His bride and ultimately it calls us to become less selfish, less absorbed in our own desires and more interested in our spouse's needs. Basically it calls us to become more like Christ and marriage is another tool which the Lord can use to transform us into the image of His Son. This undoubtedly can be very challenging at times but there are also many joyous moments and spiritual benefits to be found in this life-long lesson.

When I was living as an unmarried woman I wouldn't have said I was hugely particular about how things were done or that I had any major routines that I had to stick to. Of course there was no one else there to challenge my ways so how would I have known if I was particular when everything was done how I liked? It was very interesting for me to discover then that I can be somewhat scrupulous about certain things and ridiculously, the use of toothpaste is one of them!

Now I won't go into the details here as I'll leave that for the poem to say but the purpose of this poem is not to criticise marriage or my husband for that matter! If anything I think he comes out looking much better than I do! I've written these words in a very light-hearted tone and it's basically intended to be a humorous retelling of an event that happened over the course of about three months in my marriage. My hope is that it can provide a comical insight into the realities of marriage and hopefully others might find it as amusing as my husband and I did!

Poem

A funny observation, it's the little things in life
That often are the catalyst for marriage woes and strife.
It's frequently the petty things that really drive you mental.
To give you an example, with myself it's all things dental!

I have a simple system that I've found to work you see,
With easy steps to follow then things run efficiently!
This system went unchallenged when I lived a single life
But soon discovered this would change when I became a wife!

I'll ask if you can close your eyes whilst picturing the scene;
I'm entering the bathroom now to give my teeth a clean.
The day before this I'd observed the toothpaste running low
And so had brought a new tube in but not to use. No, no!

To place in *preparation* as the old *was* getting thin
But dearest husband clearly thought I'd put it there for him!
Deciding he'd ignore the old which still had use you see,
He ploughed into the new and left the old one there for me!

So now to finish off the old I have to *squeeze* and *squeeze*
While *he* just gives a gentle push and paste comes out with ease!
"Why bother with the old?" I hear. "Just use the new toothpaste."
But discarding it before it's done would be an utter waste!

No! The old must first be *finished! That's* the proper thing to do
And *then* we can enjoy a swift transition to the new!
The new must NOT be used before the old one is deflated
So if I find it opened then it *will* be confiscated!

And this includes the mouth wash just to clear up any query.
"Exhaust the old *then* start the new" explains my bathroom theory!
I also had a small request that's pretty fair I think;
Used floss goes IN the bin instead of draped across the sink!

Such breach of bathroom protocol upsetting my routine!
This chaos had to stop for me to keep my teeth pristine.
Deciding I would help him with this simple observation
For the sight of new toothpaste was clearly far too much temptation.

Now it wasn't like the atmosphere would bring on hypothermia
But this lack of toothpaste etiquette was giving me a hernia!
And so without a word I simply took the new away
But later with confusion, "Where's it gone?" I heard him say.

I mentioned "confiscation," well that left my husband gasping.
To find I got *this* bothered and he nearly died from laughing!
But then he showed great wisdom and decided he would listen
And thankfully he changed his ways, conceding to the system!

Such gracious compromise so now the system's not ignored,
Tranquility has been returned and order is restored.
A loving heart and listening ear would seem to be the key.
My husband demonstrated well for dwelling peaceably.

For *I* will have some habits that must drive *him* up the wall.
Of course we've yet to find one to identify at all!
Please know I'm only joking here! I'll add *that* in with haste.
I'd guess it's my obsession with the dental floss and paste!

It seems a tad eccentric to obsess like this I know
But who in their right mind would have two toothpastes on the go?
A humorous affair within our marital adventures
And soon will come the day when we debate about our dentures!

I know in life there are much more important things than this
But every little effort helps the plight for wedded bliss.
So if like me you have a spouse then please do not forget,
When sharing all things dental, *please* use toothpaste etiquette!

SCRIPTURE REFERENCES

Ephesians 5:18-21; Psalm 133:1

BOTTLE OF TEARS

INSPIRATION

My inspiration for this poem came from Psalm 56:8 which reads,

"You number my wanderings;
Put my tears into Your bottle;
Are they not in Your book?"

This verse popped into my mind one day and for some reason the image really took root in my imagination. I started to think about what a bottle of tears would look like and not just any tears, tears from an entire lifetime! I started to think things like, "How big does the bottle need to be? Will it be the same size for everyone or according to how many tears they cried in life? I wonder if we'll remember what we were crying about and whether it was worth shedding tears over?"

Part of being alive means we go through a variety of experiences and a whole host of emotions. This led me on to the think about the countless different reasons why we might find ourselves crying.

I think sometimes when we're upset it can feel like even if we tried to explain our tears to someone we'd never really be able to put the complexity of our emotions into words and truly get that person to understand whatever it is we're feeling. We'd never be able to get them to see and really feel the situation from our point of view.

This is one reason among many why I value Jesus so much. I don't even need to try and find words to express myself to Him, He already knows everything that's in my heart and understands completely what I'm going through. As Psalm 139:3-4 says,

"You comprehend my path and my lying down,
And are acquainted with all my ways.

For there is not a word on my tongue,
But behold, O Lord, You know it altogether."

With Jesus I'm never alone in my emotions and I also know that He never allows me to feel pain that He hasn't already experienced Himself. The compassion Jesus can show is truly incredible.

The more I considered the verse from Psalm 56 the more I realised it speaks of a very personal, loving God. Nobody has immunity from heartache in life but the knowledge that God numbers our wanderings, puts our tears into His bottle and writes them in His book is incredibly comforting to me. It tells me that He never takes His eyes away from me and is interested in every moment of my life. If my tears are so important that each one is recorded and stored, it tells me how deeply Jesus must treasure me in His heart.

I imagine when it comes to that day when Jesus hands me the bottle containing the tears I cried in life, only He and I will really know and fully understand the contents. Each tear will represent one of the many life stories or situations that formed and shaped my character and they'll speak of the life that we journeyed together.

POEM

To live and know emotion is a gift from God above.
We're brought into existence to discover Jesus' love.
We're beings of complexity and no two are the same
But life will bring a mixture of sheer joy and darkest pain.

A vast array of feelings to explore throughout the years
So what may be the circumstance that makes us shed our tears?
It starts with our arrival with the father standing by,
Where all can hear the wailings that declare a new-born cry.

A toddler's tears of protest as the temper hits the roof!
Or tears for countless reasons that were shed within our youth.
Sorrow as we kick against the wisdom from above,
The heartache and the pain that's caused by unrequited love.

So many different reasons bring a tear drop to the eye,
Perhaps the distant memory of mother's lullaby.
Remembering the lyrics of her long forgotten song
Or tears of sweet reunion when a friend's been gone too long.

Tears that come accompanied by raucous fits of laughter,
A joke that's shared with friends that makes you giggle for days after!
Or maybe at the cinema, a devastating scene
As star-crossed lovers bid farewell upon the silver screen.

To look within a loved one's eyes and see how much we're worth
Or weep from sheer exhaustion at the miracle of birth.
Tears of disappointment when we fail to reach a goal
Or feel we're trapped, like digging in a never-ending hole.

To find we're in an argument we've been in times before
Or tears of utter helplessness when hope is on the floor.
Tears from deep betrayal, from the broken bond of friends.
From heartache that will follow when a cherished friendship ends.

Or sitting in a hospital, hot tears may sting the eye
As yet another loved one breathes their last and says goodbye.
I think of all the highs and lows that life has brought my way
But what might be the reasons that would stir my tears today?

Tears for Jesus' sacrifice, His murder on the Tree.
Then tears of shame to realise this murder was for me.
I weep with love and gratitude for paying for my sin,
Such tears of joy I shed for my eternal life with Him.

Tears of deep despair and heavy sadness for the lost,
For those rejecting God although He paid the highest cost.
I weep in raw frustration for the spiritually blind,
For those who will ignore the truth that's there for all to find.

Tears for God's creation, at the violence on the news.
How Satan's lies distract, destroy, confound and they confuse.
Convincing man "There is no God! Just live life for yourself."
Then every moral absolute grows dusty on the shelf.

Tears at such destruction and the cruelty that I see,
A stolen child who won't return to grieving family.
Tears at such injustice, at the torment they are in
Then all that's left are tears to know the child's now safe with Him.

Such grief at worldly troubles and the reason for it all,
The tears I cry the hardest are the ones for mankind's fall.
I weep at man's rebellion and rejection of the King,
For all the pain and anguish caused by wickedness and sin.

Tears of righteous anger at the fallen state I see
And then of course I weep for all the fallen ways in me.
Tears for all the trials in this sinful flesh of mine,
For pain within my body, in my soul and in my mind.

Tears of deep regret for every hurtful word I've said,
For drifting from God's path to choose a fruitless one instead.
For turning my attention t'wards such fickle, worldly charms.
Then tears to find such grace when welcomed back with open arms.

Tears at friends' abandonment, who won't associate
With followers of Jesus whom they will not tolerate.
It hurts to be deserted when we look to Jesus' Cross
But if it's all for *His* sake then I count it all as loss.

For tears of persecution Jesus Christ Himself foretold
And everything that's stolen, He'll repay a hundred fold.
For there will come a time when every tear is washed away.
When life is tough the wait feels like forever 'til that day.

At times it feels like no-one else can understand our tears
But Jesus knows completely and can comprehend our fears.
For every battle faced, for every moment that we've cried,
We know our Saviour's there with us, He's *always* by our side.

Whatever be the reason, we can know we're not alone
For God remembers *every* tear while sitting on His Throne!
We're under the protection and the guidance of His Son,
So precious are our tears that He has bottled *every one.*

To know we're dearly treasured stirs a warmth within my heart.
He's there when we are torn by pain that makes the tear ducts start.
Our God is so attentive that He always can recall
Each precious moment in our lives for He records them all.

Tears of joy or sorrow, tears of anger, grief or strife.
How big will be the bottle that contains the tears of life?
For every one will signify a different life event.
I wonder if we'll think of every drop as tears well spent.

They'll speak of times of laughter and of sadness from the past;
A lifetime in a bottle and our stories held in glass.
Such peace there is in knowing when we knock on Heaven's door,
He'll seal the bottle, wipe our eyes, we'll shed our tears no more.

SCRIPTURE REFERENCES

Revelation 21:4

Wave Upon The Sand

Inspiration

A singer/song writer friend of mine named Harold sent me an e-mail one day in late 2012 and in his message he said that he'd been having a chat with a neighbour of his the day before. As his neighbour departed to go his way he'd called over his shoulder to my friend and said, "See Harold, there's just too much to do before I die!" Harold told me that he thought his neighbour's words were interesting and that if I could write him a poem in relation to this statement he would like to turn it into a song.

After thinking about his neighbour's comment my thoughts went towards how fast time goes by and how short life is when we look at it with an eternal perspective. When I try to consider eternity (which can be a challenging thing to do considering eternity is infinite and I have a finite mind!) I find myself trying to picture what it would feel like to have spent the earthly equivalent of 500,000 years in Heaven and yet have no less time to go again and again and again!

By comparison our time here on Earth will seem like nothing more than the blink of an eye or the click of a finger. Yet despite life's brevity this is a very important time set by God because this is when we choose where we spend eternity. Talk about big decisions! We have the free-will and responsibility to choose where our souls will go after death and this will also affect how we use our lives here on earth. We know from God's Word that death is not the end for the soul of a person, it's only the end for the body. As 2 Corinthians 5:8 says,

"We are confident, yes, well pleased rather to be absent from the body and to be present with the Lord."

I think it's very easy for people to be "busy" in life but sometimes we have to ask ourselves, "What am I busy at?" It reminds me of the

Bible story in Luke chapter ten with Mary and Martha. Martha was so preoccupied with tasks and being busy that she didn't pay any attention to Jesus whereas Mary's priority was to put herself at the feet of Jesus. It made me think how it's important in life to find that balance. Yes it's good to be busy but are the areas where we're investing our energy and time the same areas God would have us investing ourselves in? Are we bringing ourselves to the feet of Jesus on a daily basis and asking Him what He would have us do with the life that He has given us? If we're making sure that we're "about our Father's business" then our efforts will not only have an impact in this life but also in the next. It also made me think about how when we serve Jesus and His Kingdom there will always be work to be done while we're here. Sometimes life can make you feel redundant and useless but when we're in the centre of His will then we know there is always a purpose and always something to be done.

I then thought about how doing our best for God and using the resources He gives us doesn't necessarily mean it has to be something huge or impressive. Serving Him is about staying true to the life He's called us to and being sensitive to His Spirit. Making the most of things might mean a preaching ministry across land and sea or it might mean being the best child, sibling, spouse or parent we can be in the very home we already live in! The fruit will be in whatever we've been faithful to.

After thinking about these things I couldn't believe the ripple effect just one line had had in my mind. These were the thoughts that inspired me to write "Wave Upon The Sand" and thankfully Harold loved it!

My hope and prayer for this poem is that it can be an encouragement for us all to dedicate our lives to the Lord and to just commit whatever time we have on this Earth to serving the God who created us.

POEM

A breath, a wisp, a heartbeat. A vapour in His hand.
My life is but a moment like a wave upon the sand.
Compared with all eternity my days are just a few
And yet within this time there is so much for me to do.

Discovering in life both joy and sorrow I must face
And learning of the love of Christ and His amazing grace.
Among life's many lessons most important of them all
Is learning I must turn from sin and heed my Saviour's call.

For time is of the essence, I must know with certainty,
I must decide where I will dwell for all eternity.
For though the body wastes away the soul continues on
And what I do with Jesus will decide where I belong.

Will I be accepting of the God who came as Man?
Will I let Him change my heart or stay the way I am?
Will I embrace the Gospel and the truth of my Creator?
Will I use my life to serve myself or serve my Maker?

The weight of this decision is really quite profound!
With "forever" in the balance there's no time to mess around.
It's tempting to procrastinate but now the days are fleeting!
My choices must be made in life and while my heart is beating.

And so I choose my Saviour and give Him the control.
I dedicate my life to God, the One who formed my soul.
Accepting that Christ died for me and saved me from despair,
I know I'll spend forever in the safety of His care.

So now that I belong to God please use me Lord I pray,
I ask You keep me focused and attentive to Your way.
Please keep me from distractions that compete for my attention,
To make the most of every day must be my heart's intention.

For every one's a precious gift that's given by the Son,
How much I must appreciate and utilise each one!
For often it's too easy to be "busy" all the time
But energy is best applied to purposes divine.

Help me to prioritise before it is too late,
Let any impact I may have be with eternal weight.
Each moment that I live on Earth adds layers to my story,
May every choice I make in life be made for Jesus' glory.

For You have washed away my sins and cleared away my debts.
I know my heart may plan my path but You direct my steps.
I trust Your sovereign will for me, it's always what is best
And this is where I find my peace and where my soul finds rest.

Although the devil tries to make me feel like I am worthless
Now called to serve the Church of Christ each day of mine has purpose.
Whatever be my calling and whatever I may do,
I pray I stay within Your will and live my life for You.

For everything there is a time and all will have it's season,
Each purpose under Heaven has Your wise and Godly reason.
Who knows the journey I will face while following Your plan.
Perhaps I'll cross the sea or stay exactly where I am.

Considering the many ways in which I might serve You
My ministry is in whatever life You've called me to.
Whatever be assigned to me, whatever be the loss,
May I always share the Gospel and the message of Your Cross.

Fill me with compassion for the ones whose souls still thirst,
Let this motivate my spirit, help me always put You first.
So whether tasks be great or small, Lord set my heart on fire
And let my light shine brightly by fulfilling Your desire.

A breath, a wisp, a heartbeat. A vapour in Your hand.
My life is but a moment like a wave upon the sand.
So whether I have years or just one day 'til I see You,
I thank You Lord for blessing me with still so much to do.

SCRIPTURE REFERENCES

Ephesians 5:15-16

IMAGINE

INSPIRATION

The words and format of this poem were inspired by the song also entitled "Imagine" which was written by the late John Lennon. Although his death was now many years ago, the song is still very popular today and I hear it used a lot on T.V. The 2012 Olympic closing ceremony being a prime example! Whatever Lennon had in mind for the song when he wrote it, it certainly seems to have become the "atheist's anthem" in society today.

I have a huge respect for John Lennon and I share and appreciate his desire for peace and unity in the world. At the time of writing this song however, he seems to come from the view point that if mankind can "erase" God then we can achieve this unity. I find this and some other ideas expressed in his lyrics to be extremely flawed.

For example, his first two lines read, "Imagine there's no Heaven. It's easy if you try." This statement makes no sense to me. "Imagine there's no Heaven? It's easy if you try?" Why would anyone want to imagine there's no Heaven when Heaven is a place of peace, comfort, love, encouragement and where people can dwell in happiness and contentment? A place that is the embodiment of all things good, where unity reigns and loved ones are reunited. Considering unity is what Lennon longed for so much, it seems very contradictory to want to try and erase the existence of such a place.

This brings me to the conclusion that Lennon didn't actually have a problem with Heaven itself but rather with the premise on which a person might enter it. It isn't logical or in-keeping with his desire for unity and peace to then have a problem with Heaven. Rather it would seem, and this is just my opinion, that Lennon didn't take issue with the thought of eternal peace, he took issue with the thought of judgement and his accountability before God. It seems to me that

Lennon was aware of his sin and the fact that it would keep him from entering Heaven. His first line would have made more sense if he'd said "Imagine there's no judgement. It's easy if you try."

It's an understandable position and one I know I've been in myself. The thought of dwelling in Heaven is appealing but the thought of acknowledging that I'm a sinner and repenting of my sin before a Holy God is not. These are however the God-given requirements for gaining access to eternal peace.

As the Bible says in John 3:36,

> *"He who believes in the Son has everlasting life; and he who does not believe the Son shall not see life, but the wrath of God abides on him."*

Also in John 14:6,

> *"Jesus said to him, 'I am the way, the truth, and the life. No one comes to the Father except through Me.'"*

The good news of course is that God wishes that no one should perish and we can receive full forgiveness and pardon for our sins if we acknowledge them and repent of them. As 1 John 1:9 tells us,

> *"If we confess our sins, He is faithful and just to forgive us our sins and to cleanse us from all unrighteousness."*

The Bible explains very clearly that as a result of our own sin and rebellion we are born spiritually separated from God and we'll face Him as our righteous judge one day. A terrifying thought. Thankfully God being a God of love as well as righteousness hasn't left it there. He's provided us with a way where we never have to face Him as our judge because our sins have already been dealt with. We can attain this free gift of grace just by trusting in His Son Jesus Christ and accepting that all of our sin has been paid for through His sacrifice on the Cross. We need never fear or face judgement because our God has already dealt with it. To ignore this wonderful provision is a tragedy because to accept it is to have freedom and liberation from not only the fear of judgement but also from judgement itself.

It's clear Lennon was imagining an end to conflict and war. To do this however we have to recognise the source responsible for all conflict in the world and that blame belongs to Satan. Therefore the only way strife will ever truly come to an end lies in the hands of the only one who can defeat him, Jesus Christ. As I mentioned earlier Lennon seemed to hold the view that the belief in the existence of God or "religion" as he confused it with, led to conflict amongst mankind and therefore to "erase" God would be to erase conflict. The problem doesn't lie with God however, it lies with mankind.

Firstly, there is a huge difference between "religion" and having a relationship with Jesus. These two things are often confused but are hugely different. Secondly, God exists whether we choose to believe in Him or not and thinking that by erasing all acknowledgment of Him will improve human nature and behaviour is a huge mistake. He's the One who created us and He's the One who died to pay for our sins. Ignoring this fact will only cause more chaos and heartache for everyone.

If there's no God then there's no authority to say what's right and wrong or what's true or false. If someone decides it's ok to kidnap and murder a child who are we to tell them that's wrong if truth is relative? Who says it's wrong to murder? If we all make up our own truths, live by our own moral code and do what's right in our own eyes then it's just one person's opinion against another. To me that's a frightening thought. Erasing God from our society is not the answer, embracing Him is.

The Bible shows us that this kind of behaviour has happened before as Judges 21: 25 says,

"In those days there was no king in Israel; everyone did what was right in his own eyes."

Proverbs 16:25 warns us of the consequences of this,

"There is a way that seems right to a man, but it's end is the way of death."

The subject matter in Lennon's song runs so deep that really the lyrics only touch the tip of the iceberg and so too does my poem.

He was clearly a great thinker and part of me feels that his song "Imagine" was in fact related to his interest and search for God.

There seems to be an on-going debate as to whether he was a Christian or not before his tragic death in 1980. I read an interesting article written by Jesse Carey who is the Interactive Media Producer for CBN.com. His article reveals that an interview with Lennon was unearthed in recent years. It took place in 1969 for a segment on a Canadian Broadcasting Corporation show and gives some very interesting insights into Lennon's thoughts and feelings towards Jesus in the years leading up to his assassination.

An excerpt from the article quoting the interview says this,

> *"And though this is the first time many Beatles fans have heard this particular conversation, Lennon's interest in Christ was no secret in the early '70s. In his book, The Gospel According to the Beatles, writer Steve Turner said that there was a period in his life when the world's most famous songwriter deeply wanted to know who Jesus was. According to the book, in an effort to escape the chaos of public life, Lennon would often retreat to television and became a regular viewer of the era's most influential evangelists including Billy Graham, Oral Roberts and even Pat Robertson.*

In 1972, Lennon even took part in a written correspondence with Roberts, in which he apologised and further explained his statement about being "bigger" than God. The Beatles frontman, who had experimented with a variety of drugs and spiritual ideas wrote this to Roberts:

"The point is this, I want happiness. I don't want to keep on with drugs. Paul told me once, 'You made fun of me for taking drugs, but you will regret it in the end.' Explain to me what Christianity can do for me. Is it phoney? Can He love me? I want out of hell."

Oral Roberts sent him a long response, giving him a copy of his book Miracle of Seed Faith and a detailed explanation of God's love for him.

Five years later, in 1977, Lennon became deeply moved by NBC's broadcast of the movie Jesus of Nazareth and told his friends that he had become a born-again Christian. A week after seeing the film,

Lennon returned to church on Easter Sunday with his wife Yoko and son Sean in tow."

The article goes on to talk about the difficulties Lennon faced after professing Jesus Christ as his Saviour and although it may seem like he fell away from Christianity, we know that if a person truly has given their heart to Jesus then they belong to Him eternally no matter how far behind they may fall in their walk with Him. He is faithful even when we are not and after all, we don't have eternal life temporarily!

I deeply hope to see Lennon in Heaven one day where there is no war and no "religion" too; only the peace and unity that he longed for on Earth. Thankfully peace is also the desire of Jesus and I look forward to the day when He brings an end to sin and it's consequences once and for all. Only then will the whole world really and truly in the words of Lennon, "Live as one."

POEM

Imagine there's no Heaven.
No comfort when we die.
We'll never see our loved ones
No matter how we cry.

Imagine all the people, grieving life away.

Imagine there's no justice.
No moral wrong or right.
If there's no God above us
Then who's to say who's right?

Imagine all the people, living life their way.

You may say I'm a dreamer
But this doesn't sound like one.
Godless lives won't unite us.
They'll reap sorrow for everyone.

Imagine no possessions.
How long would you survive?
You'll never try to regain them
As long as you're alive?

Imagine all the people, fighting every day.

You may say I'm a dreamer
But this ain't kidding anyone.
There's no point in pretending
Without God we can live as one.

Imagine there's a Heaven.
It's easy if you try.
A place where love unites us
And conflict says goodbye.

Imagine all the people, living eternally.

You see I'm a believer
And when the final days have come,
Peace will reign through our Saviour
And the world will live as one.

SCRIPTURE REFERENCES

Revelation 21:3-6

Beautiful Exchange

During a trip to the U.S.A. to visit some relatives, my husband's Aunt Carol said she was preparing a women's Bible study and would be teaching on Isaiah 61:1-3. The verses read,

"The Spirit of the Lord God is upon Me, because the Lord has anointed Me to preach good tidings to the poor; He has sent Me to heal the broken-hearted, To proclaim liberty to the captives, And the opening of the prison to those who are bound; To proclaim the acceptable year of the Lord, And the day of vengeance of our God; To comfort all who mourn, To console those who mourn in Zion, To give them beauty for ashes, The oil of joy for mourning, The garment of praise for the spirit of heaviness; That they may be called trees of righteousness, The planting of the Lord, that He may be glorified."

Carol said she loved how the verses talk about the beautiful exchanges the Lord gives us such as "beauty for ashes," "the oil of joy for mourning" and "the garment of praise for the spirit of heaviness." She said she would love to have a poem with this theme to accompany her sermon and wondered if I could write one for her. What a challenge!

I spent some time reading these particular verses and praying over them and as I did, I started to consider some of the different exchanges the Lord has brought into my life since I gave my heart to Jesus in 2006. The first and most important exchange being eternal damnation for eternal salvation! That in itself is amazing and blows my mind!

The more I thought about His power and presence in my life the more I realised how many levels God can reach me on. It's not just me of course, everyone who opens up their heart and life to Jesus can find the power of the Holy Spirit doing wonderful things within them! I wanted to share this amazing truth with people and by the grace of God I found myself writing "Beautiful Exchange."

POEM

Oh wretched creature that I was, so far from God's intention.
To think that I ignored Him when my life was *His* invention!
Denying the importance of the hands that formed my being
Would reap such deadly consequence and rob my life of meaning.

My spirit yearned for truth to which this world could never cater
And empty is the heart that won't acknowledge it's Creator.
My eyes and ears were opened to the sin of my rejection.
I realised my image is in fact my God's reflection!

Such knowledge too profound, to be created in *His* likeness!
And through the Cross of Christ I can be viewed by God as righteous.
I praise my mighty King for I no longer face damnation,
Through Jesus' sacrifice I now rejoice in sweet salvation!

Redemption that's secure and now my soul's no more adrift.
I traded death for life by just accepting Jesus' gift!
Eternity re-written and my future re-arranged.
I praise His awesome power! What a beautiful exchange!

Wisdom and discernment He can now impute to me.
I gave my heart then Jesus gave me brand new eyes to see!
When blinded by my sin the Bible seemed to be absurd
But now that I belong to Him I'm awestruck by His Word!

My life is now for Jesus, I embrace a brand new start
And feel His Holy Spirit start to work within my heart.
I'm now a new creation as the past has been erased
And as I walk with Him I learn how much can be replaced!

For even if I think of wasted days within my story,
He turns those times around and now can use them for His glory.
For though I uttered not His name, His light refused to see,
Today I testify of how He kept a hold of me.

When living in rebellion, a lonely path I trod
But now I'm warmly welcomed in the family of God!
Without our Saviour, we would have in common not a thing
But now I'm blessed by countless friends, connected by our King!

Empowered by the Spirit, He has turned my life around.
Transforming mind and motive, hardened views thrown upside down!
Refreshing my perspectives, gaining help with sin's removal,
No longer seeking man's acclaim but rather *God's* approval.

Instead of fear and emptiness where worries never cease,
I seek His Godly counsel, gaining joy and inner peace
And in the midst of trials when I feel I'll fail the test,
My weakness only proves His strength and swaps my strife for rest.

He overcomes my helplessness when fear would have me frozen
And gently He reminds me I'm secure for I've been chosen!
In life are many twists and turns but with my God's direction,
Despair gives way to hope for I am under His protection.

Daily He renews me as I humbly seek His face
And though I'm "work in progress" I am covered by His grace.
His love completely changed me and His truth transformed my days.
On bended knees I bow my head and offer up my praise.

A lost and hardened heart that only Jesus Christ could change,
I'm grateful He provided such a beautiful exchange!
We all can have redemption if we listen for His voice,
He's calling out to everyone and gives us all a choice.

Conviction of the heart is like His spiritual nudge.
We can greet Him as our Saviour or we'll face Him as our Judge.
We must consider soberly this spiritual matter,
He longs we choose the former and avoid facing the latter!

God's will is none should perish and that's why He sent His Son;
The blood of Jesus Christ was shed to cover everyone!
There's room enough for all within this strong and mighty Tower
And no-one is beyond Him, there's no limit to His power.

He turns the stricken into rescued, the accused He justifies.
The lost become the found and truth prevails instead of lies.
There's comfort and encouragement for all who've been rejected.
With purpose, place and meaning, all condemned can be accepted.

Endowed with Jesus' pardon, He can heal our brokenness.
He fills a hardened heart with praise, uprooting bitterness.
Refusing all involvement with a cold dictatorship;
Rejecting our "religion," we embrace relationship!

Selfishness to selflessness, He counters lust's desire.
Removes the need for sweet revenge and quenches fury's fire.
His faithfulness is crystal clear when life provides a shock,
His promises hold fast and turn the quicksand into rock.

The God who cares for every need, provides our daily bread,
Who's counted each and every hair that grows upon your head!
A Saviour deeply personal, whose love cannot be measured.
We go from insecurity to cherished, loved and treasured.

If you don't know your Saviour may I take this time to say,
He's waited for you patiently so give your life today!
He will not disappoint you for you're *His* unique creation.
He's given you freewill to choose and *now* is the day of salvation!

It doesn't matter what you've done, with Christ you'll be a winner
For He's a bigger Saviour than you'll ever be a sinner.
There's not a heart or soul on Earth that Jesus cannot change
So trust your life to Him and start *your* beautiful exchange!

Scripture References

2 Corinthians 5:17

FREEDOM OF SPEECH

INSPIRATION

It seems to me that in life everyone is entitled to their opinion. Everyone except the Christian that is. I've experienced persecution personally in my own places of work and also witnessed it in general life and different situations.

The enemy's attack on God's people certainly seems to be building in intensity and it's becoming harder and harder to be a Christian in this world. I know Christians have been persecuted all throughout history and countless people have been martyred for their Christian beliefs. The angle I'm coming from in this poem though is the position of a Christian living in Britain in the current times. Our formerly "Christian Nation" is now becoming so adamant and hateful in it's fight against God and even the belief in His very existence. People are now being mocked, pilloried, humiliated and shamed into silence just for standing on basic Biblical truths and wanting to apply these to their lives.

One example is the fact that many schools are now teaching children very anti-Christian principles in the classroom and parents are coming under extreme pressure for wanting to teach their children about Biblical truths in the home. I've also watched as MP's stand up in Parliament and voice a differing opinion to the common view and one that dares to be founded in Biblical doctrine only for that person to then be denounced as a "bigot." The next day they're being forced to publicly back track on their words or face losing their job.

If we are no longer allowed to have freedom of thought or freedom of speech then we are no longer living in a democracy and are dwelling under a dictatorship. I once heard Pastor Mike McIntosh say that if the system is persecuting or putting a person in jail for the views that person holds as a Bible believing Christian then the system has gone too far. No one has the right to try and control another person's mind.

Now I know that many people may argue and say that over the years "Christianity" has often been like a dictatorship and tried to control people but that is not Jesus and not true Christianity. To know Jesus is to know God and to know Him personally and have a relationship with Him is totally different to being under the dictation of "man-made religion." When we know Him as our Saviour we experience first hand how loving, caring, forgiving and kind He is. God has graciously given us all the option to decide for ourselves whether we'll look to Him as our Saviour or not, He will never force us to love Him and so He has given us all the gift of free-will. Any example that suggests otherwise is not true Christianity and is a tragic misrepresentation of Christ by sinful mankind.

The point of my poem is not to start an argument or to come across as belligerent or angry, it's simply to make the point that as a human being who has made an educated and informed decision, I have accepted that Jesus Christ died to pay for my sins and He is my personal Saviour. I don't demand that everyone else agrees one hundred percent with everything about my life or else must be labelled with all sorts of ugly names. I simply ask for the freedom to live my life as a Christian and be allowed to form my own opinions based on what God's Word reveals. All I am asking for is equality and freedom of speech.

POEM

Don't tell me I can't worship Jesus,
Don't tell me I can't speak His name.
I'm not asking *you* to keep quiet,
I'd be grateful if you'd do the same.

Don't curse me for having convictions
That differ to those in your heart.
Just because I follow Jesus
Doesn't mean you can tear me apart.

Although our opinions may differ
And our views show a noted division,
This does not permit scornful actions
Where beliefs are then met with derision.

You say we must all have our freedom,
To ourselves we must "Always be true!"
If I'm pilloried for my opinions
Does *that* sound like freedom to you?

You demonstrate views that are hostile
To the God and the faith I belong
But though you may find it offensive,
Doesn't mean to say that it's wrong.

You say you want love and compassion
To rule and to reign in this life
Yet you contradict this with *your* actions,
Showing hatred and stirring up strife.

Your anger is quickly awakened
When learning our views don't reflect.
If I just nod along like a robot
Would you *really* give me your respect?

If I didn't hold fast my convictions
And was silenced to speak not His name,
Would I then earn your favour and kindness?
Do you only respect those the same?

Because I don't share your opinions
Then "tolerance" is what *I* must lack.
When shouting me down for opposing,
Are *you* showing tolerance back?

You call me a dumb ignoramus,
To your "wisdom" you think I should bow.
When I don't then you call me a bigot
So who's being ignorant now?

When you throw at me insults and curses
With damaging words that can slice,
If you hate me because I'm a Christian,
Then you must have a phobia of Christ!

Now this doesn't make me dislike you,
It just means that our views disagree
But I show *you* respect and compassion.
So I ask, please don't disrespect me.

You voice your opinions quite clearly,
It's "your right" to your freedom of speech
But I must be shamed into silence,
So you rob me *my* freedom of speech.

You tell me my thoughts are old fashioned
And to "move with the times" would be clever
But God does not change with man's thinking
And the truth of the Lord stands forever.

Your views disagree with the Church's
So you say it should change "to be fair"
But if you don't believe God's existence,
Then why do you protest or care?

If God isn't real then why bother?
Just to claim every path has been trod?
But why then acknowledge the building
When you won't be acknowledging God?

To me this is simply dogmatic.
Your hypocrisy I can't perceive.
Insisting that sin be accepted
By the God in whom you don't believe.

Now God wishes no-one should perish,
In our places He suffered great loss.
Now we're all welcomed into His presence
But we *must* leave our sins at the Cross.

But you tell me that God has no placement
And His wisdom applies not to you.
You may not accept His existence
But don't disrespect those who do.

So don't tell me I can't read the Bible,
Try to force me to share in *your* views
For I will stay true to my Saviour
No matter what's said on the news.

Though Governments say to "move forward"
And even if man gives the nod,
The system might say it's accepted
But it won't be accepted by God.

For He is above our opinions,
He won't bow to the secular view.
We can see from the Bible and history
That man's wicked ways are not new.

We may try to remove every mention
Of His name and each Heaven-bound nod.
His acknowledgment might be abolished
But this will not eradicate God!

His Church does not change at man's calling,
To think that it should is absurd.
It does not require "updating"
For it's built on the truth of God's Word.

I'll stand on this truth for my lifetime
No matter if you disagree.
You say you've endured "persecution"
But oh how you persecute me!

You shout in my face for my tolerance
But it's perfectly clear you want more.
You also *demand* my endorsement
And to leave my beliefs on the floor.

But I humble myself before Jesus
And I listen each day for His voice.
I don't make demands you do likewise.
I respectfully honour your choice.

God never will force us to choose Him,
It's the free-will He gave to mankind.
So we all have the right to decipher
And the right to control our own mind.

Though my faith means I'm labelled as "stupid,"
I am blessed with a brain which I use.
So don't tell me I can't be a Christian
And deny me *my* freedom to choose.

For my faith isn't "lack of intelligence"
And although our opinions don't link,
In Christ I take every thought captive
So do not tell me what to think.

Understand I don't judge your decisions,
Your beliefs are completely your choice.
I ask you accept mine are different
And like you, have a freedom to voice.

So for me, come hell or high water,
Come insults as sharp as a sword,
I'll always bow down to my Saviour
And I'll *always* declare "Christ is Lord!"

SCRIPTURE REFERENCES

Isaiah 40:8

THE MEANING OF EASTER

INSPIRATION

It was just after Easter 2013 when I felt inspired to write this poem. Over the month leading up to this Christian festival I witnessed various different statements and comments which I felt were a real reflection of how society is trying to omit Jesus more and more from our culture and nation.

The poem is intended to vary between humour and a more serious tone, sometimes with direct explanations related to Easter and other times with mere suggestions that will hopefully raise intrigue for further research!

My prayer is that it can be a reminder for us all to look beyond the fluffy chicks, chocolate eggs and cute bunnies and remember or perhaps discover for the first time what the true meaning of Easter is.

POEM

Tulips, bunnies, fluffy chicks appear in fullest force
But can I find an Easter card that represents the source?
With shelves of chocolate eggs that could outsize the average head,
It seems that Easter greetings come with rabbits on instead.

I don't begrudge festivities and colour in my day
But cannot help but feel that Easter's point is stole away.
Are children being taught of *why* they have two weeks off school?
Or is it just two weeks of sweets, escaping teacher's rule?

Now let's address "Shrove Tuesday" where one might indulge one's self
As pancake mixes disappear off every market shelf!
But what's the *point* in feasting on this mix of milk and flour
A month before "Good Friday" and the Saviour's darkest hour?

As Easter time approaches I hear people asking questions
And witness some responses and some very strange suggestions!
"What's the deal with pancakes? Who remembers what that meant?
What's Jesus got to do with giving up some stuff for lent?"

"I'm giving up the chocolate and the booze for forty days!
A proper bit of detox ought to help me in my ways.
I'll pride myself on "self control" and tick that off my list
Then when those days are up I'll self indulge for what I've missed!"

Now why would you deny yourself and go to all that trouble
If just to brag of "self control" and then consume in double?
This special time was set aside for inner contemplation,
A time for fellowship with God and self-examination.

A season to re-focus with God's help to tame the flesh.
With humble prayers of penitence the spirit is refreshed.
Or "What's "good" about "Good Friday?" Why's it special? What's
the fuss?"
Well "Good Friday" is the day our King died on a Cross for us!

He pardoned us from every sin and once that's understood
It's very clear to see *why* they declared this day as "good!"
But commercialism's influence has made the meaning worthless
And nations can forget their God and Easter's very purpose.

My heart is saddened every year as Jesus is erased,
By chirping chicks and chocolate eggs my Saviour's been replaced.
Though Easter greetings come complete with bunny ears and tail,
These symbols are as hollow as the chocolate eggs for sale.

It seems that now "The Holidays" must serve the non-believer
For Santa's not the purpose or the point of Christmas either!
Now this won't make me popular and may make some see red
But Easter is the time when Jesus Christ rose from the dead!

This message may offend and put some noses out of joint
But Jesus' Resurrection *is* the core of Easter's point!
It's existence lies with Christ and His achievement is the reason
We have an extra long weekend and celebrate the season!

To think about Palm Sunday when they sang His praise with Psalms,
At Christ's Triumphal Entry all the crowds laid down their palms.
This act declared His deity, His Lordship over all!
Within a week He'd pay the price for sinful mankind's fall.

For He endured betrayal in a garden dark with night.
This sinless Man was seized as each Disciple fled in fright!
He stood before accusers who did all they could to shame
His purest motivations and deny His holy name.

They dressed Him up to mock Him, stripped away His dignity
And all this He endured so you and I could then go free.
They beat Him to a bloody pulp and tied Him to a post.
Resigned, He chose to die to save the thing He loved the most.

With every lash upon His back His body weakened more
Yet His resolve to save His Bride grew stronger than before.
With nails and ropes confining the Messiah to the Tree,
What *really* held Him there was deepest love for you and me!

His purpose on the Earth, to seek and save that which was lost.
Providing man's atonement, God *Himself* covered the cost!
This makes it such a tragedy when Easter is diminished
When Jesus' final words upon that Cross were "It is finished!"

Achieving what mankind could not to save *us* from despair!
The curtain in the temple tore and earth shook everywhere!
Graves were opened, rocks were split! Bystanders stood quite awed.
Seeing these signs the guards declared, "This *was* the Son of God!"

Three days He lay entombed and then the angel rolled the stone.
Defeating death, in glory rose to reign upon His Throne.
Fulfilling every prophesy, He crushed the serpent's head.
No longer cursed by death, we have eternal life instead!

"Hosannah!" is the Easter song my grateful heart will sing!
Acknowledging what He achieved I praise my awesome King!
So now consider Easter chicks and bunnies everywhere.
I hope I've illustrated why these things just don't compare!

Perhaps a little truth may lie in some of them per se;
The egg, a simple symbol of the stone that rolled away.
But fluffy, pagan symbols that are favoured by the media?
For answers on traditions, we can find on Wikipedia!

But ignoring the real reason is a mistake we can't afford
So this Easter look to Jesus, He's our Saviour and our Lord.
Though chocolate eggs may beckon, take a moment to recall.
Indulge yourself with Jesus, *He's* the sweetest Gift of all!

Scripture References

Mark 16:4-7

To Do What You Do

A song writing friend of mine e-mailed me a few days after the tragedy of the Boston bombings in 2013. The identity of the people responsible was still unknown at this time and my friend asked me if I could write some lyrics for him in reaction to this terrible event.

He also asked if I could write it as if the person or people responsible for the bombings were right there in front of me and to think of the questions I would like to ask them in regards to their actions. I wrote this poem in response to his request.

Poem

So now that your ways are accomplished and you've washed all the
blood from your hands
Would you please take a moment to reason for your actions I can't
understand?
Why is it you long for destruction? With visions of evil you've toyed.
Why do you thrive on the suffering and the pain in the lives you've
destroyed?
Families are robbed of their children, this heartache caused only by *you.*
What if sorrow was brought to *your* doorstep? Does *your* family mean
nothing to you?

But to do what you do, there's no reasoning with you.
And I pray for the ones that you hurt.

Your actions are hateful and spiteful. In whose name do you fight? For
whose sake?
Regardless of what you believe in, their lives were not yours to take.
Do you think we'll now hear your opinions and respect your position
and cause?
If these are your means to express them then *why* would we listen
or pause?
Clearly you're filled with a hatred for the race to which you belong to.
Is the darkness of your heart's desire to make all just as angry as you?

But to do what you do, there's no reasoning with you.
And I give my frustration to God.

My flesh wants to show you no mercy and to know that you'll pay for
your sin
But the Lord wishes no one should perish and all has been paid for
by Him.
It challenges me to accept this when your actions brought others
such loss
But I know we can *all* find forgiveness when we kneel at the foot of
the Cross.
So I'll pray you repent from such evil though this damage cannot
be erased.
You've caused devastation and sorrow, taking loved ones who can't
be replaced.

When you do what you do, there's no reasoning with you.
Yet I know Jesus died in your place.

So whatever your reasons or motives, whatever the point of your plans,
Your wickedness goes not unnoticed and vengeance belongs in
His hands.
So I'll look towards Heaven for comfort and find peace knowing He's
in control.
I'll pray for the ones who are suffering and conviction to enter
your soul.
I yearn for the day strife is ended and all sorrow has said it's goodbyes.
Until then we can all seek His comfort and find healing for
heartbroken cries.

Though you do what you do, I know Christ will come through.
And I pray His return would be soon.

SCRIPTURE REFERENCES

Proverbs 3:25-26; Proverbs 30:5; Psalm 29:10-11; Revelation 22:20-21

The Palm Tree

It was in May 2013 when I attended the "Manna Conference" at "Church On The Way" in Bradford, England. I heard Cathie Simpson, wife to Pastor David Simpson of Calvary Motherwell, teach a sermon on encouragement.

During her talk she mentioned the Palm Tree and how it bends in the wind and doesn't break like other trees. In contrast, the Palm Tree is flexible, digging it's roots deeper during a storm and after it's been through some turbulence it becomes stronger than it was before.

Cathie used this analogy to compare the tree in a storm to our "storms" of life. She encouraged us to dig our roots deeper into Jesus when we're going through tribulation, knowing that He will give us the strength to weather the storm and will bring us out at the other side stronger than we were before. I thought this was a lovely picture and felt inspired to write a poem.

Poem

Let me be like the Palm Tree
That bends with the storms of life
When billowing winds have descended
And I'm pounded and beaten by strife.

Let me bow in the force of such fury
Though I'm challenged right down to my core.
Like the Palm Tree I'll dig my roots deeper
Seeking depths that I've not sought before.

Though the storm keeps on forcing me lower,
My security will be approved
For I'm rooted and grounded in Jesus,
So I know that I will not be moved.

In my weakness His strength will be proven
As my life remains rooted in Him,
So I'll bend but not break from this onslaught
As He comforts my soul from within.

Though it feels like there's terrible damage,
This hardship has purpose and reason
For I know that my Saviour is with me
And this trial is only a season.

When turmoil at last has blown over
And the calm of the day is restored,
I'll stand taller and stronger than ever
Having seen through the storm with my Lord.

For a faith that has met with resistance
Is a faith that is stronger and true.
So when storms come again, I know Jesus my Friend
Will be there and His love will shine through.

SCRIPTURE REFERENCES

2 Corinthians 12:9

THE GRAVEYARD

INSPIRATION

One summer's evening in June 2013 my husband and I paid a visit to his Grandmother and Grandfather's graveside. I had never been to the graveyard before and this poem is inspired by my experience there.

Although these words address the harsh reality of death, my intention is not to bring spirits down with this poem but rather to offer hope and peace for our hearts in the face of the cold truth. My desire is to bring glory to the name of Jesus Christ who faced and defeated death on our behalf and in doing so, bought us all eternal life. When we know Jesus as our Saviour we can know with absolute assurance that death is not the end, it is in fact just the beginning.

POEM

I walked one summer's evening through a gateway made of stone
And quietly I ventured down a gravel path unknown.
With warm and dappled sunshine gently peeking through the trees,
The sweetened smells of summer floated softly on the breeze.

A grassy slope of monuments rose silently ahead.
With solemn dignity they spoke of each eternal bed.
The peaceful scene lay basking in the pleasant warmth of day,
Disturbed by crunching footsteps as I carried on my way.

At the bottom of the hill I saw a sight that stole my breath
For children lay beneath these stones, too young to witness death.
The decorated, tiny graves of baby girls and boys
Had offerings of cards and gifts and lonely, unused toys.

The echo of a mother's cry was present in my ears
As death denied her of her child, replacing them with tears.
A sudden surge of sorrow overwhelmed my saddened heart
When "Born Asleep" declared their end before they saw the start.

Blinking back the tears I started walking up the hill,
With every stone and epitaph I faced more sorrow still.
For there engraved in gold I'd read a message and a name,
Each one a testimony to the family's grief and pain.

"Here lies…" "In loving memory…" "The day they fell asleep…"
The plot on which bereaved would kneel to mourn their loss and weep.
Grieving for their dearest ones who time would not give back
With flowers full of vibrant life against the marble black.

These colours stood in contrast to the sorrow of the scene
But soon they too would fade with time which no-one can redeem.
I noticed different details of each grave side that was there,
The statues and the trinkets that were placed with loving care.

A woman of just twenty one had dragonflies with wings,
They sparkled in the sunlight with her other favourite things.
Another showed a rose motif, a family's sign of duty.
Inscribed across the bottom, "You're Forever Our Sleeping Beauty."

Some of them had photographs with life behind the eyes,
An image in a frame before they'd said their last goodbyes.
A golfer's pose or clarinet engraved beside a name;
Reflections of each character and no two were the same.

Scriptures on a headstone said they'd entered Heaven's Gates,
The story of their lifetime now confined between two dates.
No plaque to tell me what they'd done or who had gained their love.
The finer details gone and only known by God above.

I saw that further on there stood the graves of olden days,
These weather beaten tablets had no flowery displays
For those who'd known *their* names had to their own graves
been invited,
So I pictured them rejoicing in the Heavens, reunited.

As I gazed upon the graveyard staring straight at death's reality,
It served a stark reminder of my own fragile mortality.
Surrounded by memorials, the truth there to embrace;
The young and old, the rich and poor *will* meet death face to face.

To look upon this scene of countless headstones in a row
And see the darker side of life we were not meant to know.
The weight of our rebellion that *caused* all sin and death
Crushed me like a monolith and took away my breath.

For this was never meant to be, it wasn't Jesus' plan.
We should have stayed forever in the safety of His palm.
We never would have seen decay or sadness from goodbye,
We never would have had to watch a loved one slowly die.

So now we try to deal with death but we do not know how
For we should not have known the devastation we know now.
We're sentenced to a life that's filled with sorrow in our heart,
It should have had no placement but it tears our souls apart.

This nearly overwhelmed me as I stood amongst the stone
But then I thought of Jesus Christ and how He left His Throne.
He left to face this very cause and break this wicked hold;
He dealt our *sin* a deathly blow as prophesies foretold!

We may place religious symbols at the grave of one we've lost
But Jesus covered *every* base by dying on the Cross.
Our Saviour paid for every sin and every wicked deed.
To enter into glory, faith in Christ is all we need.

He swallowed death in victory! O' death where is your sting?
This knowledge gave me hope and peace that only Christ could bring.
He bought us all eternal life and banished all uncertainty
For if we're known by Christ our names are written in eternity.

I started to retrace my steps and wiped away a tear,
So grateful for our Saviour's love that leaves nothing to fear.
Once more I passed the tiny graves, those babies free from harm.
The children death denied of life now safe in Jesus' arms.

In realms that have no shadows, they're now basking in God's Son.
My sadness now combined with peace, I left them in the sun.
I realised with comfort as I walked through evening air,
One bright and golden, sunny day, dear ones, I'll meet you there.

SCRIPTURE REFERENCES

Matthew 5:24; 1 Corinthians 15:20-22

A DAILY WALK

The summer of 2012 was the beginning of a very difficult season for me due to severe physical trials. I had gone from being a highly active person, performing in eight shows a week to someone whose movement was extremely restricted and I was in constant pain for months on end. I soon discovered that a battle with your body can quickly turn into a battle with your spirit and also your mind. Some days just getting to the end of the street was like climbing a mountain for me.

Going through such a fiery trial I decided to read through the Psalms every day and found them to be wonderfully real and encouraging. Another particular part of the Bible that I found comforting was Lamentations 3:22-26 which reads,

> *"Through the Lord's mercies we are not consumed, because His compassions fail not. They are new every morning; great is Your faithfulness. "The Lord is my portion," says my soul, "Therefore I hope in Him!" The Lord is good to those who wait for Him, to the soul who seeks Him. It is good that one should hope and wait quietly for the salvation of the Lord."*

At the time of writing this poem it was one year on from the start of this very painful time and I can honestly say that if it hadn't been for Jesus, the family and friends He put around me and people lifting me up in prayer, I don't know where I would be now. It was without a doubt the toughest year of my life on many levels but through this season I was more aware than ever of how God is my Rock, my Fortress and my daily Salvation. He taught me that I can trust Him with my life and I must take things a day at a time. Although I can't see the purpose behind all of these things I know that He can and all He asks is that

I take His hand every day and walk with Him, knowing that He's in control and has my best interests at heart.

My hope is that this poem can be an encouragement to anyone who might be going through a hard time in whatever manner it may be. As Christians we're not exempt from hardship and sorrow but we have a Saviour who has only allowed the trial to come our way because He has the strength to get us through it. I've learned that if I try to take on the problems and issues of tomorrow or any further down the line, it gets overwhelming.

God's grace is sufficient for the day and this is something I have learned to be absolutely true. It's also something that I have to remind myself of daily and continually apply to my life. I'm not claiming to have got it all down pat now and that I never battle with things anymore, not at all. It's an ongoing trial and it's a daily walk but anything that drives a person to the feet of Jesus is a positive thing ultimately. It's good that I'm reminded daily that I need my Saviour and as Micah 6:8 tells us,

"He has shown you, O man, what is good; and what does the Lord require of you but to do justly, to love mercy, and to walk humbly with your God?"

I don't know what the future holds but I follow the one who does know. I have peace knowing my life lies in the hands of the God who created me and there's no other place I would have it.

Wherever you may be today and however you may be feeling, I'd like to encourage you to trust your future to Jesus too and just keep your eyes on Him. If you're already a Christian then the power that put the moon and the stars in the sky, created all life and brought Jesus back from the dead is the same power that works within you and in your life. No matter what your circumstances may be, when you know Jesus you're always in good hands and we can do all things through Christ who strengthens us.

POEM

Upon this day a year ago a journey new began.
My eyes could see the steps ahead, my heart had made it's plan
But things did not go easily no matter how I tried.
I could not win, regardless of how many tears I cried.

I watched as all I'd worked for simply crumbled all around;
My dreams and aspirations now lay broken on the ground.
Each day my body failed me deep despair would strike afresh.
My youth and freedom gone, I was betrayed by my own flesh.

So many nights my sleepless eyes stared blankly at the dark,
The weight of tribulation on my soul had left it's mark.
Thinking of the lifestyle I no longer could attain,
A prisoner of my circumstance and caged in by the pain.

My every motion crippling, each movement now a chore.
My life became a shadow of the one I'd had before.
It seemed that I was destined to endure the darkest path,
The joy within me stolen, I'd forgotten how to laugh.

To think of me a year ago and know what lay ahead,
I do not envy me, I'm glad I'm in *today* instead.
If You'd shown me what awaited I'd have fainted there and then
Yet somehow here I stand, prepared to face each day again.

For daily You renewed me with a strength not of my own.
Though times were dark indeed I did not face those days alone.
Your tender mercies covered me and pulled me from despair.
Upheld by Your right hand, I knew I dwelt in safety there.

Submitting to Your will for me and doubting not Your love,
Creator of my soul, I sought Your comfort from above.
Your thoughts are not like my thoughts and my ways are not Your ways.
Dwelling on Your goodness I could trust You with my days.

Remembering Your promises, the Scriptures came to life!
Learning truths I would not know if I had not known strife.
Searching through Your Holy Word, it brought my spirit food
For every situation works together for my good.

You're bigger than my circumstance, Your power has no limit.
My situation proves Your strength sustains me every minute.
Your peace surpasses knowledge, in myself I cannot boast
For when I fail to seek You Lord is when I hurt the most.

If I neglect Your counsel seeking other things instead,
I lose my way as thoughts distort for You're my daily bread.
I must remember who it is that I am talking to
For desperation only strikes when I lose sight of You.

To focus on the problem then I start to lose perspective.
The loss feels overwhelming when I think in retrospective
But every day I have a choice, a thought I must implant,
To see the things I *can* do instead of those I can't.

Though one year on and still my body struggles to get by,
I know You always understand, my precious God on high.
You meet me in whatever depths I call upon Your name,
This battle is on-going for so too is the pain.

But You've shown me I can trust in You though life will bring
me sorrow
And keep my focus on today, not trials of tomorrow.
You've blessed me with compassion from my family and friends.
My gratitude for their support will never come to end.

Each day I journey onwards though I don't know what's in store,
My spirit rests in knowing that You'll meet my needs and more.
Your grace is all sufficient, You're my ever faithful Friend.
My joy was merely hiding for You've helped me laugh again.

No matter how we plan in life, success be near or far,
I've learned we're never in control, we merely think we are.
It's You who plans my path O' Lord with strength to see me through
And when each day comes to it's end my praise shall be of You.

My eyes will look to Heaven though my flesh be put to shame,
Whatever lies ahead let me bring glory to Your name.
Relying every morning on Your mercies that are new,
I'll take You by the hand Lord for my daily walk with You.

SCRIPTURE REFERENCES

2 Corinthians 12:9; Philippians 1:6; 1 Peter 5:10; 2 Timothy 1:12

CANDY CANE

INSPIRATION

As I was taking down the decorations after Christmas 2013 my Mother-In-Law started to tell me about the Christian symbolism behind the candy cane and I was completely intrigued by what she said. Although I had seen the popular confectionary every year during the Christmas season, I had never realised that it had Christian meanings in it's origins. I decided to read up about it online and discovered that there are some mixed reviews as to the meanings behind the candy cane.

Whether this Christmas treat truly has it's beginnings based in Christianity or not I'm not sure, nor do I think it's hugely important. After all, it is only a sweetie! The real meaning of Christmas however will always be about the birth of Jesus Christ and I felt that even if the Christian symbolism was added to the candy cane in later years, it was still a great opportunity to write a poem and share the true message of Christmas.

One thing is for sure, from now on whenever Christmas comes around and I see those red stripes wrapping around the white candy cane, it'll always turn my thoughts towards Jesus Christ and the blood my Saviour shed for me.

POEM

I see you little candy cane, a cheery Christmas sight!
A gentle curve of peppermint with stripes of red and white.
A simple little festive treat, I've seen you times before.
I hear you have a secret though, your presence means much more.

Your core is made of vibrant white, a symbol there to show
That Christ was born of virgin birth, His life was pure as snow.
You speak of how His back was flogged with three slim stripes of red.
A thicker stripe that spirals down says Jesus' blood was shed.

A challenge for the dentures, you're a hard and chewy treat!
The goodness of the Gospel found within your taste so sweet.
Your firm and solid density may give the jaw a shock
But this reflects God's promise, He's our Refuge and our Rock.

I find your shape intriguing as a slender pole and hook.
Your form can tell a story just as well as any book
For if I turn you upside down what message do you say?
You mark the name of Jesus as I see the letter "J."

But when you stand with head held high and hanging from your hook,
I see a reassuring shape just like a Shepherd's crook.
For we like sheep had wandered far and all had gone astray
So Jesus the Good Shepherd came to save and show the Way.

I thought you'd kept your meaning to yourself quite sneakily
But you wear your every symbol like a coat for all to see!
I realise with every twist you glorify God's name.
A peppermint delight, what a clever candy cane!

Although there are the sceptics who say you are a fake,
You wouldn't be the *first* to be denied for Jesus' sake!
Take comfort little candy cane, it isn't you they mock;
It's the One you represent and He's the *Everlasting* Rock!

Though some deny your origins they have not eyes to see
But now *I* know your tale it's what you'll always mean to me.
So thank you little candy cane for all the truth you bring.
Proclaim your Christmas message, Jesus Christ the Risen King!

Scripture References

Luke 2:6-20

Nothing Compares To Thee

Inspiration

One evening I was feeling particularly wearied by the ongoing trials of life. As I retreated to a quiet room to have some time seeking the Lord through His Word and in prayer, I found myself humbly asking Him, "A word of encouragement Lord, please!"

As I began to study the Scriptures I was reminded that as Christians we are just "passing through" this life and our trials and tribulations are not permanent. As I meditated on this thought I began to think about the wonderful day when I'll get to see Jesus face to face and was thinking about how much I long for this. When it comes to my heart's desire, nothing compares to the thought and the knowledge of this moment. In all honesty, I think waiting for it feels a lot like being homesick at times. My soul longs for my Saviour and for the trials and cares of this world to be a thing of the past.

As I sat there thinking about this I began to write "Nothing Compares To Thee." I think the first verse of this poem clearly reveals the weary place I was in at this point. As I continued to write however, I found myself going through a process with the Lord and my focus and attitude shifted to a much more upbeat and positive one. One of strength, purpose and with a drive for life. As I wrote, the trials began to dim and shrink in size as God ministered to my soul, encouraged my heart and got my focus back onto Him and His purpose for my life.

I wrote this poem from beginning to end in one sitting and by the end of it I felt like I had been through some kind of therapy session! I felt rejuvenated, inspired and refreshed and I think this is reflected in the journey and attitude of each verse. I could see the truth of Matthew 11:28-30 where it says,

"Come to Me, all you who labor and are heavy laden, and I will give you rest. Take My yoke upon you and learn from Me, for I am gentle and lowly in heart, and you will find rest for your souls. For My yoke is easy and My burden is light."

Jesus never promised us an easy road in life but He did promise He would never leave us or forsake us, He would be with us right to the end and that when the end comes we will have eternity with Him. The more I thought of the eternal, the more I felt the desire and urgency to share the truth of the Gospel while I still can.

It was the spiritual boost I had needed and Jesus really did answer my initial prayer that evening. He encouraged me, fed me, lifted me up and got me refocused and back on track in my perspectives. Time spent with Jesus is always fulfilling and this along with countless other reasons is why for me, nothing compares to Him!

POEM

Nothing compares to Thee O' Lord, nothing compares to Thee.
I yearn in my heart for Your blesséd embrace
For nothing compares to Thee.
I long for these trials and troubles to end,
To come face to face with my Saviour and Friend.
As pain melts away my spirit will mend
For nothing compares to Thee.

I hunger to be next to Thee O' Lord, I hunger to be next to Thee.
I know in Your presence all sorrow is gone
So I hunger to be next to Thee.
The woes of this burdensome, troublesome life
Can weary my soul and cut like a knife
But knowing they're temporal frees me from strife
As I hunger to be next to Thee.

I pray I can be more like Thee O' Lord, I pray I can be more like Thee.
The more I consider the lost of this world
The more I pray make me like Thee!
I see every day as the enemy strives,
Encouraging people to lead godless lives.
To think of Your Gospel my spirit revives!
I'm inspired to be more like Thee.

I long for others to know Thee O' Lord, I long for others to know Thee.
Awake to the truth that eternity calls,
Yes I long for others to know Thee!
Whatever my number of days that remain
To live will mean Christ, to die will be gain.
With every last breath I will worship Your name!
For I long that others should know Thee.

I always find comfort in Thee O' Lord, I always find comfort in Thee.
A time will come when all labour will cease
And I always find comfort in Thee.
For though I am weary I lift up my face,
Direct all my praise to Thine Heavenly place,
Find joy everlasting from Thy Throne of grace.
I always find comfort in Thee.

Nothing compares to Thee O' Lord, nothing compares to Thee.
You strengthen my spirit and bolster my heart,
No nothing compares to Thee.
You know all my fears and hear every prayer,
You love me completely and show me You care.
You'll be with me here until I can be There,
O' Lord nothing compares to Thee.

SCRIPTURE REFERENCES

2 Corinthians 4:8-10; Psalm 86:6-13

THE WOMAN ON THE WALL

INSPIRATION

This poem describes one particular day in my life during the summer of 2014. I had some important auditions coming up and so was on my way to a singing lesson with lots of material to learn when the inspiration for this poem was brought into my life. My hope and prayer is that these words may speak to the heart of anyone who is yet to know Jesus as their personal Saviour.

POEM

Awoken from a blissful sleep, I groan and turn away.
Before me lie the challenges of yet another day.
Never one for mornings, my eyelids feel quite stuck
But I've over used the "Snooze" alarm and so I must get up!

My day begins with old routines and soon I'm out the door,
Plough headlong into battle with the London crowds galore!
The siren of an ambulance goes screaming down the street
As I duck and weave my way around a million pairs of feet.

With people from all walks of life and faces from each nation
I run this crazy gauntlet as I journey to the station.
I pause to find my platform and then scurry off again,
I swiftly swipe my Oyster Card and jump aboard the train.

I inwardly rejoice at empty seats to sit upon
And feel I've won a prize to find the air conditioning on!
With closing doors and whistle blows, we slowly pull away.
A gentle sigh escapes my lips as I escape the fray.

Before too long I'm taking in the views of London scenes,
The building sites and rows of houses crammed in like sardines.
Noticing with interest as I'm peering through the glass,
Those blessèd few with garden space! A patch of muddy grass.

Yes London can be costly but it has so much to give!
A bitter sweet existence in the town I choose to live.
A melting pot where people come, pursuing hopes and dreams.
I too arrived with starry eyed ambition in my teens.

The life that I have led, I wouldn't trade it for another
For the city kept it's promise though we sometimes hate each other!
Rich with opportunities where prices are insane,
The pace of London life not far behind my speeding train!

An automated voice declares we've reached my destination
And so I disembark and make my way out of the station.
My mind already racing with the tasks I must recall
And this is when I notice her, a woman on a wall.

She sits with no companion with a blank look on her face.
She silently observes the street while sitting in her place.
Her day is quite in contrast to the hubbub of the city.
My curiosity awakes with sorrow more than pity.

I realise with sadness there's a fact I can't ignore;
I've made this journey several times and seen her there before.
No matter what the time of day or if it's rain or shine,
Her days are spent upon this wall. She sits there all the time.

I struggle with this thought for when I look at her I see
A fellow human being. She's a woman, just like me.
We may have different histories but now our journeys meet.
Today our paths have crossed for we're both here on this street.

I don't know if she had a dream or plan for life at all
But I don't believe she hoped to spend her days upon this wall.
Who knows the details of the maze that led her to this place.
I think of what I'd say if we were talking face to face.

I'd like to say hello to you, enquire how you are.
I'd ask you what your name is and if you've come from far.
I'd listen to your story, all the things you'd have me hear.
The journey of your life so far and how you've ended here.

I wouldn't want to patronise or say things to offend,
I'd ask you out of interest and approach you as a friend.
We'd have a conversation where no judgement would be found,
I'd share with you the simple truth that turned *my* life around.

The truth that pulled me from despair and filled my heart with hope,
That showed me what life's meaning is and gave me strength to cope.
The news that set my spirit free, released my soul from strife.
The truth that Jesus has a plan and purpose for each life!

You may have heard His name before and think it's just a "hook"
But I'd speak about our God and ask you take a second look.
Our time on Planet Earth is not a "cosmic accident."
The day we're born is *planned* by God and not coincident!

To know our Maker means that we need never feel alone.
Do you know that Jesus formed you in the secret place unknown?
Created in *His* image, you're His special work of art!
His fingerprint within, He signed His name upon your heart!

You're made because God loves you and has plans for you to do
And not only were you made *by* Him but made *for* Jesus too!
Created so that you could spend eternity with Him!
Would you let the greatness of His love transform your heart within?

Deep down perhaps you wish to be the best that you can be.
The gateway to that life is God and Jesus holds the key!
He knows your capabilities, your strengths and talents too.
With Christ your skills will flourish for *He gave* those gifts to you!

I'd speak about His grace and how He died to save us all.
I'd share with you His Gospel as we'd sit upon the wall.
I'd talk about the love He's shown by dying on the Cross,
The vict'ry He achieved for us I couldn't get across!

For now no matter what we've done, no matter where we've been,
We *all* can find forgiveness and the slate can be wiped clean!
No "scrubbing up" is needed or "disguise" to make us "ready."
We can't disappoint or shock Him for He knows it all already!

We needn't feel unworthy to approach His Holy Throne
For He waits with open arms to welcome *all* His children home.
I'd tell you this with confidence, with no uncertainty.
I *know* that this is true because it's what He did for me.

I'd ask if you *could* start again would you seize the chance?
Would you open up to something new and maybe change your stance?
Perhaps you're quite content and wouldn't want to change a thing
Or maybe you would *love* to see the wonders He can bring.

No problem is too big for God, no circumstance too bleak.
He can turn your life around, provide the answers that you seek.
I'd ask you if there's anything that's standing in your way
And then I'd ask you let it go and give your heart today!

This world can't offer anything that takes the place of Him,
No drink or drugs or fancy cars can fill that void within.
When *I* began to look to God, responding to His call,
I battled with my fears and doubts and wrestled with them all.

I thought of all the worldly things that held my admiration
But realised *they were not worth* the trade of my salvation!
The treasures of this fallen world will only leave you empty.
They cannot buy eternal life where blessings flow aplenty!

I may not know of *your* concerns but one thing is the same,
Our God above is calling you and Jesus is His name!
He longs to set you free, you won't be caged in by "religion."
A personal *relationship* with Jesus is *His* vision!

The thought of change is daunting or to know where to begin
But give your heart to Jesus and then trust the rest to Him.
Who knows the plans He has for you but whether big or small,
He'll fill your life with purpose and He'll guide you through it all.

He sees the possibilities, the doors He can unlock.
Instead of bricks and mortar set your life upon the Rock.
Make this day a special day, a day you won't forget
When you made the *best* decision. It's a choice you won't regret.

His power could transform you if you'd only let Him in.
Your life so dear He **died** for you now will you **live** for Him?
Of course I've only pictured how our conversation goes.
Would you *want* to sit and chat to me? Only Jesus knows.

My tasks today demand I dwell no longer on this street,
Perhaps I'll get to share these words next time our journeys meet.
I'll pray He might prepare you to respond to Jesus' call
And thank the Lord He led me to the woman on the wall.

SCRIPTURE REFERENCES

2 Corinthians 6:2; Psalm 139:13-16; Psalm 95:7-8; Psalm 119:73;
1 John 4:19; Romans 5:6-10; John 10:10; John 15:16

AFTERWORD

After writing this poem I took a copy with me every time I went for a singing lesson in the hope I may get to share it with the lady who was my inspiration. Sadly I never saw the woman on the wall again. I remember her in my prayers from time to time and hope she's doing better now wherever she is. I'm confident Jesus knows exactly where she is and has His eyes on her.

I would certainly advise practicing caution when approaching strangers on the street but if this poem can be used in any way to reach a lost soul then it would be an answer to my prayers. An acquaintance of mine said he was going to take it with him when he goes out ministering to the homeless in his area and that was a huge blessing for me to hear.

In reality though we don't need to be literally sitting on a wall every day for these words to apply to us, it could be metaphorically speaking too. Many people have great jobs and full social lives but feel they're going nowhere in life. I was one of them before I gave my life to Jesus! My prayer for this poem is that it may guide any lost soul out of hopelessness whatever their social status may be.

TO LIVE IS CHRIST

One day during some Bible study I read Philippians 1:21 which reads,

"For me, to live is Christ and to die is gain."

I've read the Apostle Paul's words here many times before but for some reason they really stuck out to me on this particular reading. I started to think about how profound his statement is and it acted as a reminder to me that as a Christian, I need to be giving the reins of my life over to God on a daily basis and sacrificing any selfish ambition.

When faced with the challenges of life, my desire to try and control things can sometimes creep in and so to read that my life belongs to Christ is a great reminder that He is in control. My reason for living is not to pursue my own agenda but rather to make myself available to God and let Him use me in whatever capacity He sees fit. It was like a gentle reminder to desire God's will and His plans for me above all else in life.

I then went on to think about the second half of the verse and how it really contrasts with the worldly view of death. Death is of course a painful and devastating part of life for all of us but the secular view is that it's the end of the journey and the beginning of oblivion. At the very least death is viewed as entering into the unknown.

Not so for the Christian however as we read in this verse that for those who have put their faith in Jesus, to die is gain! When Christ is who you live for then death doesn't separate you from Him, it takes you to His side. 2 Corinthians 5:8 confirms this when it says,

"We are confident, yes, well pleased rather to be absent from the body and to be present with the Lord."

Whatever we may serve in life, if it's anything other than Jesus then death will bring an end to it and we'll experience it's loss. If we live to serve money then we'll lose it the moment we die and it will belong to someone else. If we live for fame and glory that too will be forgotten in time and we'll have no connection to it in the afterlife. If we live for our relationships and family members then sadly death will bring an end to that too.

The only one who can actually say they have anything to gain when they die is the Christian. Only the person who has said "To live it Christ" can say with any assurance "To die is gain." The power of these words really spoke to me. It got me thinking about how we have Heaven to look forward to and eternal life in the presence of Jesus! A very different view point indeed.

Paul's words certainly reflect my heart's desire to be with my Saviour but of course it's not a battle between life and death in this verse but rather a comparison between serving Jesus in this life and then being united with Him in the next. It's the joy that the Christian has in using their time on Earth to serve God combined with the promise and assurance of enjoying fellowship with Him in Heaven. Before long I found myself writing this little poem to capture my thoughts and feelings.

POEM

"To live is Christ, to die is gain." The challenge of this statement!
To live to serve *another's* name when "self" wants no abatement.
To live is *Christ*! Not "me" nor "I," not "mine" nor selfish will.
To live is *Jesus*, God on High, *His* purpose to fulfil.

Yet once a sweet surrender's found what offers more reward
Than feet that walk on solid ground in service to our Lord?
What purpose could be greater or what calling more divine
Than one to our Creator stating "Not *my* will but Thine?"

Then comes the second trial where we hear "to die is *gain*."
When the hands upon the dial stop, will *we* feel the same?
For all who said "to live is Christ" can die with true assurance.
Their perfect Saviour sacrificed can give this reassurance.

Our lives on Earth are all we know yet weakness ends when
Heaven bound!
The Christian *gains* in letting go, a notion that is most profound!
Though ever willing to remain, in life and death we worship Him.
This hope our spirits can't contain, to be united with our King.

Scripture References

1 Thessalonians 5:9-10

FIELD OF SOULS

INSPIRATION

Between the 17th of July and the 11th of November 2014, a major art installation was placed around the Tower of London to mark the one hundred year anniversary of the first full day of Britain's involvement in the First World War. Created by artists Paul Cummins and Tom Piper, there were 888,246 ceramic poppies placed within the Tower's famous moat with each poppy representing a British military fatality during the war. It was on the 9th of November that year that my husband and I decided to visit the exhibition and witness for ourselves the dramatic views that the poppies created.

After my initial thrill and awe at the vibrancy and sheer volume of poppies, the magnitude of the losses suffered during the war began to really hit me. As I stared at the poppies and considered what they represented I suddenly didn't feel like I was looking at a field of flowers anymore but rather I was staring at a field of souls. It was this thought that inspired me to start writing my poem.

POEM

A cold afternoon at the Tower of London, skirting the puddles and patches of mud.
I gaze at the vision of red that's before me, the colour of passion, the colour of blood.
Thousands of poppies now stand to attention, lovingly crafted with no two the same.
A flower for every soul lost in the battle with each representing a face and a name.

One for each father who fought for his children, who thought of their
future when on the front line.
One for each son who in uniform proudly, kissed Mother farewell and
said he'd be fine.
Poppies that speak of the hard working women, the daughters and
mothers, the aunties and wives
Whose service was rendered while nursing the injured. The brave men
and women who gave up their lives.

They fought for our freedom, for king and for country. The future of
Britain was worth fighting for.
The heart of each poppy as black as death's shadow, as black as the
hearts at the root of the war.
I ponder a thought as I stare at the poppies and vividly picture a scene
in my mind.
I think of the tears of their mothers and children, the harrowing grief of
those left behind.

What if the flowers were solitary symbols and each represented a *tear*
that was shed?
This river of crimson would rush over Britain and every last inch would
be covered in red.
The battle was won but there were no winners. The victory came at a
staggering cost.
They fought a good fight and did what was needed but now we will
always remember the lost.

I think of another who died for our freedom, another who fought with
the darkest of foes.
I picture the Cross at the place called Golgotha, the place where
another red river flows.
War was declared in the garden of Eden as sin and creation became
intertwined.
A battle that needed a mighty Redeemer who'd fight for the prize- the
souls of mankind.

The cruellest of enemies seeking mass slaughter whose merciless
rampage would only get worse,
Who'd laugh in the face of an army of thousands! No guns or grenades
could have lifted the curse.
The victory lay on a *spiritual* level, this battle was not just with flesh
and with bone.
One had the will and the strength that was needed. No one could win
this but Jesus alone.

I think of the conflict surrounding His mission, the barrage of warfare
He faced from the start.
The forces of hell that were working against Him but couldn't contend
with the love in His heart.
The rumours surrounding His very conception, His Mother presumed
to be caught in her sin.
The cries of her labour were heard from a *stable!* The Saviour of *all*
found no room at the Inn.

The birth of the Boy who would be the Messiah, Herod breathed
murder on hearing the news!
His life already in perilous danger, the Babe who was born to be King
of the Jews.
The Creator of all came to save His creation! Enduring the hardships
and sorrows of man.
He battled fatigue and every temptation but never digressed from
fulfilling His plan.

Through blistering heat He earnestly travelled, healing the sick and
seeking the lost.
Constantly dealing with false accusations yet speaking God's truth
whatever the cost.
Always contending with man-made religion, opposing corruption and
"rules" of the day.
Exposing the Pharisees' lies and deception while showing His people
the trustworthy way.

Then came the ultimate test of His Spirit, marking the start of His
loneliest time;
Deep in the garden He cried to His Father, "Nevertheless, not *My* will
but Thine!"
Jesus endured the harshest betrayal, faced His arrest and arduous trial.
Bearing the beatings, the scourging and mocking. To rescue His people
He'd suffer each mile.

He watched His Disciples disown Him completely, rejected by man as
He hung on the Tree.
The fiercest of battles this world has witnessed, when Jesus Christ died
to save you and me!
The God of the Universe entered the trenches and thought of *His*
children to fight to the death.
Our great Liberator, unstoppable Champion fought as a Man and gave
every last breath!

This battle Christ won and *we* are the winners! He conquered the grave
and defeated death's claim.
The greatest of victories won by our Saviour, now every soul born can
be saved by His name!
Let's give God the glory, rejoice in this triumph! May all our praises
rush forth like a flood!
Let every heart on the Earth give Him honour for every last inch has
been drenched in His blood.

Now we await the final of battles for soon comes the day as
the Prophets foretold
When Christ will return to set up His Kingdom, take hold of
the dragon, that serpent of old.
Oh this will be a war like no other as Christ will appear as bright
as the sun!
How we rejoice in the victory promised for Jesus our Saviour has
already won!

Praise to our God, all you His servants and those who fear Him, both small and great!
The ending is written with Satan defeated! Chained to the pits and bound by hell's gate.
How the heart yearns for Jesus' arrival! Keenly awaiting the First and the Last.
Bringing the end to sin and destruction, rendering warfare a thing of the past.

Steadfast we wait for that glittering future, behold He is coming to rule His domain!
The grace of our Lord Jesus Christ be upon us, sing Alleluia! Forever He'll reign!
So as we live for our King in our country let's show our respect and not be denied;
Remembering those who died for our freedom by gratefully wearing the poppy with pride.

SCRIPTURE REFERENCES

John 15:13; Revelation 19:11-14

THE THIEF

One day my husband told me about an acquaintance of ours who had undergone an operation on his back and was struggling to recover. I was suddenly overwhelmed with compassion for this man and also felt quite a strong sense of sorrow and frustration for his predicament.

As one who has struggled with my own health issues I was surprised to find I was suddenly transported in my thoughts back to some very dark and difficult times during painful physical trials. I began to recall how debilitating the pain was in my life and found myself thinking with anger, "Pain is such a thief! It robs you of so much!" I was soon writing down my thoughts and my poem "The Thief" is the result of this.

My hope for the first part of this poem is that it may be able to offer an honest insight into what it can be like living with chronic physical pain. It's a hard thing to understand until you've experienced it first hand. My words and descriptions may differ to what another sufferer might express or feel but it's how I've felt at times and so hope it can offer even just a little insight into the limitations and frustrations pain can bring.

My prayer for the second part of this poem though is that it can hopefully bring a message of encouragement and strength. As a Christian I know I am far from immune to pain and suffering in this world but I also know that whatever I face in life I face it with Jesus. He is faithful. He can hear the voice of one who is weeping and He understands the liquid prayers of our heart.

No matter what we go through in life He is with us and working things out for our benefit. It may not feel like that at the time but we don't go on what we "feel" in life, we go on what God has shown us and promised us through His Son Jesus Christ and by the Holy Word of God. The things Satan would use to tear us down, God can use to build us up.

Jesus loves us, He cares for us and is always with us, enabling us to deal with whatever trials come our way. We can have victory through Him in every circumstance we face in this life and we know we have the ultimate victory through Him in the next.

If there is anyone reading this poem who is perhaps suffering with chronic pain of any kind be it physical, mental, or emotional, I'd like to encourage you today. You are not alone. There are people who understand what you're going through and Jesus understands better than anyone. He endured the worst kind of pain, more than we will ever know.

If you already know Jesus as your Saviour then I'd like to encourage you to keep your eyes on Him. Call out to Him, whisper His name in your heart and He will be there. He is able.

If you don't know Jesus personally yet then I'd like to take this moment to ask you to change this. The Bible tells us that when we seek God with our whole heart then we will find Him. Seek Him this day I urge you. Your Saviour waits for you and is more than able to help you in your time of need.

Not only will He give you the strength to endure and possibly overcome whatever it is you're currently going through in this life but He will cover you with His grace and seal you with the promise of eternal life. Eternal life in a place where there is no pain, no suffering, no anguish, no heartache, no tears and no more broken bodies or spirits. You have nothing to lose and everything to gain! Seek Him dear friend, He is able.

POEM

Robbed of my freedom and robbed of my youth,
Pleading with Heaven above.
Asking for respite from Satan's attack;
He'd have me believe I've been robbed of Your love.

Robbed of my livelihood, robbed of my dreams,
Turning my memories sour.
Slicing my flesh with invisible knives
While making each minute feel like an hour.

Robbed of my character, robbed of my joy,
Bidding farewell to my skill.
Stripped of a passion I've had all my life,
Dictated to daily and robbed of free-will.

My body complaining at every request
As if I'm much older in age.
No longer able to hope or to plan,
Resigning myself to life in a cage.

Watching the colours of joy disappear,
Replaced by the saddest of grey.
A life that was thriving now merely exists
As each aspiration slips further away.

So who is this thief that robs me of much?
Should I dare mention it's name?
Relentlessly torturing body and mind;
My dreaded companion, the one they call pain.

A powerful monster that never needs rest,
Whose presence is most uninvited.
A beast that won't tire or leave me in peace,
Whose interest in me is most unrequited.

With talons so piercing and teeth that devour
It silently gnaws at my soul.
Unable to picture my life before pain;
A darkness that threatens to swallow me whole.

And yet there is one who cuts through the black
With light that continues to shine.
A candle that faithfully flickers away,
A powerful source with a presence Divine.

My Sovereign Companion the Lord Jesus Christ
Causes my spirits to lift.
Knowing He's with me brings peace to my soul
And soon I can feel my thoughts start to shift.

Robbed not of His mercy, robbed not of my Shield,
Hope burns in my heart like a fire.
For I know the One in whom I believe
And soon He reminds me the devil's a liar!

Robbed not of my Saviour and not of His care,
Robbed not of my vict'ry in Him!
Robbed not of Christ's promise that *He'll* be my strength,
Robbed not of my faith nor the love of my King.

Salvation secure in the work of the Cross,
His counsel brings peace to my soul.
Robbed not of eternity next to my God,
Robbed not of the knowledge that He's in control.

Comfort and solace found only in Christ,
His grace is sustaining my days.
Robbed not of His help in my time of deep need,
Knowing my God is *still* worthy of praise.

Trusting His mercies are new every morn,
Pushing these troubles afar.
Though my soul wishes to cry "All is well!"
To cry "Thou art with me!" is better by far.

Close to my Saviour, relying on Him,
Robbed not of my fervour to pray.
Delivered through freedom found only in Christ,
Restoring the years that were stolen away.

So much in my life the thief cannot touch,
Things Jesus has promised to me;
One day I'll receive my heavenly form
And sing "Hallelujah" for then I'll be free!

SCRIPTURE REFERENCES

Psalm 6:6-9; 1 Peter 1:6-9; John 14:16; Matthew 28:20; Psalm 7:17;
Joel 2:25

Until We Meet Again

Inspiration

I was attending a family funeral in May 2015 and as I sat through the ceremony I was thinking about how sad death is. No matter what the circumstances are at a funeral, no matter how young or old the person may have been, the loss of a loved one is a tragic and difficult event to handle in our lives and process within our hearts.

I began thinking about how the only comfort and hope we have in these situations is the fact that Jesus is risen. If we don't set our focus on this then sorrow and despair can definitely threaten to overwhelm us. The more I felt the pull of sadness on my heart the more I felt it was imperative to counter this inner pain with focusing on the truth of the Resurrection. It's here that we have the promise of life after death as well as the promise of being reunited with those who have gone before us in the faith. What a wonderful peace this can bring to a heart that is grieving.

I then began to consider how it's through no works of our own that we can attain eternal life but purely by the work of the Cross. It's solely by accepting that the Crucifixion of Jesus Christ paid for the sins of the world, including our own sin! It's only by putting our faith in Him as our personal Saviour that we are granted access to Heaven. This then led me to think about how funerals can often cause people to consider their own spiritual standing and be more open to discussing things to do with God, death and the afterlife.

I started to feel inspired to write a poem that could be used by many to commemorate the loss of a loved one. I really wanted this poem to offer the truth of the Gospel as well as bringing comfort to those who mourn. I pray that my poem "Until We Meet Again" can be even just a sliver of light on what may otherwise be a very dark day.

POEM

We're gathered here together in honour of your life,
To celebrate our memories of you
For every person present is a soul that you have touched,
In ways that only *you* knew how to do.

We all could tell a story or share an anecdote,
Remembering the details of your days.
Each tale a small addition to the picture of your life
That moved so many hearts in different ways.

Our memories may comfort as we fondly reminisce,
For now we face the sorrow of our loss
But though we miss you dearly there's a peace within our hearts,
For Jesus won your freedom on the Cross.

We know that you accepted Him as Saviour and as Lord,
We know that you received His gift of grace.
The soul that trusts in Jesus will not be cast away
But warmly welcomed home by His embrace.

The God of all creation now holds you in His arms!
His good and faithful servant has come home!
Redemption through your faith in *His* achievement on the Cross
And so we boast in *Christ* and *Christ alone.*

All glory, praise and honour we rightly give to Him,
His death and Resurrection we proclaim!
We know you have salvation through the work that *He* has done
So now we glorify His holy name.

Your feet will now be walking through those shining streets of gold,
Your days within eternity begin.
Your eyes have seen the Saviour! Your ears have heard His voice!
What joy there is to picture you with Him.

And so as we commemorate your life with gratitude
Our hope is in the promise of His reign.
One day we'll reunite and we will *never* say goodbye;
We'll hold you dear until we meet again.

SCRIPTURE REFERENCES

Psalm 116:15; Matthew 25:23; Matthew 5:4

DEAR MR ATHEIST...

INSPIRATION

I started to write this poem in August 2015 as I had been hearing quite a few very heated opinions coming from some well known and outspoken atheists who are in the British public eye. What I found interesting is that they frequently like to voice their displeasure and their judgement on the actions of other human beings and often in a rather aggressive and vitriolic way.

I found myself thinking that some of the views expressed seemed to contradict each other and that their opinions on the character of God were so far from the truth. I soon found myself inspired to write a poem and compose it in the form of a letter as I really felt in my heart that I would love to communicate and have a respectful conversation about the views expressed. Ultimately though I would love to share the Gospel with them just as others once shared the Gospel with me!

POEM

Dear Mr Atheist, good day to you I say!
I hope you're keeping well for winter's swiftly on it's way.
We've had a lovely summer though, a welcome change indeed!
A warm and pretty autumn now I'd say is what we need.

Enough about the weather though and on to other news!
I see you here and there and I've been listening to your views.
You have me quite perplexed by an inconsistency.
I wonder, would you spend some time and reason through with me?

I know that in the public eye the pressure must be great
But still, you seem quite confident in voicing what you hate.
You're very clear and open with your disbelief in God
And seem to think theistic views are dim and rather odd.

Of course, we disagree on this but I will not insist.
You've every right to have your faith that God does not exist.
Oh yes dear Mr Atheist, a faith it is for sure!
It's just your chosen system in which you feel secure.

I'm sure you'll have your reasons and use them as defence
But sometimes preconceptions are displayed as "evidence."
Perhaps you say it's "logical" and firmly based on "fact"
But history and science would declare this inexact.

Don't you think it's possible that often people choose
To only see the "evidence" that fits in with their views?
The point though Mr Atheist as I have discussed,
You say there is no God and this is where you place your trust.

So going on this premise, as far as I can see
You hold to "evolution" as how we came to be.
The thought of a Creator is a tale to bid farewell,
We're all the random product of a solitary cell.

We're just a bag of chemicals that slowly over time
Has sprouted fins then legs and arms, evolving from the slime.
Implying life is meaningless we logically conclude
The Universe has no design, no evil and no good.

For if there's "good and evil" then there *must* be moral law
But if there's no Law *Giver* then there is no moral law!
This means that life's a "free for all," it's "each man for himself!"
The rules of "right and wrong" must now be left upon the shelf.

We do what makes us "happy," it's our basic right and liberty
To do what's pleasing in *our* eyes with no accountability.
"Truth" is what we make it and there is no "absolute."
Though if we're absolute on *this* then *that's* an absolute.

But looking from your viewpoint and seeing life your way
I really am surprised by what you said the other day.
I see you get upset at those who hunt and kill for fun,
With hounds and horns a'blaring it's a thrilling sport for some.

This cruelty makes you livid though and fills you with such fire.
You speak against their actions with a passion to admire.
You fight to change the laws and bring in fairer protocol
Which leads me to conclude you *do* seek justice after all.

I'll state just for the record that I actually agree
For wickedness and cruelty are unbiblical you see.
I too despise injustice and I don't condone their choice
To brutalise the weaker or those without a voice.

But the problem Mr Atheist, if what you say is true
That "truth" *is* only relative, it's only true for you!
This cancels your authority or instinct to condemn;
Although it may be *vile* to you it's simply sport to them!

You cannot get upset at this, *your* message after all
Is "live our lives as *we* see fit, our preference makes the call."
Although your moral compass says these acts are deeply cruel
You have no grounds to say that this *must be* the standard rule.

You don't have the position to rebuke those you despise.
Like you, they're simply doing what is pleasing in *their* eyes!
If behaviour is determined by mindless molecules
Then altruistic notions would break evolution's rules.

To show another kindness we can go to any length
But "natural selection" only favours those with strength.
Our DNA knows *nothing* about caring for the weak,
"Survival of the fittest" means to dominate the meek.

So listening to your message which you preach with such conviction,
To claim our acts are "good or bad" is quite the contradiction.
For either we "evolved" and we live life for ourself
Or God exists and "right and wrong" *must* come down from the shelf.

But if you base your lifestyle on the laws of evolution
"You have no right to judge" must be the logical conclusion.
And yet you say it's terrible so *why* do you dismay?
Is it wrong because it's cruel or is it just because *you* say?

Why would your opinion have dominion over others?
You're just one "bag of chemicals" dictating to another!
I'm sorry Mr Atheist, it doesn't work that way.
I ask you to invest a bit more thought in what you say.

You've taken it upon yourself to tell us right from wrong
But moral absolutes and evolution don't belong.
It's *God* who gives us boundaries and shows us what is right,
With wisdom He conveys to us what's pleasing in His sight.

Ignoring our Designer you admire His design.
You preach that we should love while blocking out the source Divine.
It seems though Mr Atheist despite your godless case,
Your confidence in self suggests you'd like to take His place.

You value rather highly your opinions and your stance;
If offered God's position then I think you'd seize the chance!
You seem to have no issue telling others what to do,
You just don't like authority when ruling over you.

You love to tell us how to think with views that never budge
But why are you the one in charge and who made you our judge?
I'd like to make it clear my point is not to make you cross
But please appreciate that this is how you come across.

You say the realm of animals includes the human race
But when it comes to *people* you show very little grace.
Considering your message is that *love* is what we lack
You seem to just reserve *your* love for those who don't talk back.

This harsh, berating attitude will close the ears of some
For those who *dare* to differ feel the sharp edge of your tongue.
But insults only weaken and devalue your position;
Perhaps a more respectful tone for those in opposition?

We don't do well to dictate that "all *must* think like me!"
I'm sure you can concur it's not a crime to disagree.
But let's return a moment to the views that you express
For here there lies a query that perhaps we could address.

We know that evolution says survival shows no care
So morals and a conscience *have* to find their roots elsewhere.
Perhaps my next suggestion might make you feel a traitor
But could it be that "inner voice" has come from your Creator?

Inherently we *know* that love and justice are correct,
It's why we feel enraged when someone shows *us* disrespect.
God's given us a conscience and awareness right from birth;
Created in *His image* we possess intrinsic worth!

But recognising God exists you claim is just naive.
You say that He's a "fairytale," a "myth" or "make believe"
And though you mock His followers this act is nothing new,
You simply join the many who have mocked before you too.

The thing is Mr Atheist, we must address forthwith,
Me thinks thou dost protest too much if God *is* just a "myth!"
Indifference seems more logical than hate and vitriol.
This does suggest dear friend you're not an atheist at all.

For if you *truly* don't believe then you won't waste your time
And yet you dedicate your life to scoffing the Divine.
No one argues endlessly on matters non existent
But when it comes to Jesus Christ you're really quite persistent!

The way you go on tirades it's as if your soul's afflicted.
For one who says they "don't believe" you're really quite convicted!
You cannot *stand* the thought that we're accountable for sin;
It's not that you're an atheist but rather you *hate* Him!

You *hate* to think that God exists or say the Bible's true.
Your problem isn't disbelief but what this *means* for you.
And so you dig your heels in to make sure you advance;
In order to defend your life you must sustain your stance.

But this is such a tragedy, if only you would see
The God you curse and hate so deeply, *died* to set you free!
The animosity you show is really undeserved.
Despite the Saviour's *love* for you He makes you feel unnerved.

What's interesting to note is when it comes to other "gods"
It seems it's only Jesus Christ with whom you are at odds.
May I suggest a reason as to why this is the case?
I think deep down you know that He's the *One* you'll have to face.

The others do not challenge you, they do not pose a threat.
You say "same goes for Jesus" with your public views and yet
It's *His* name that you curse so much, it's clear He bothers you.
Could it be dear friend that it's because His words are true?

When Jesus said "I Am the Way, I Am the Truth and the Life"
His words cut through the hardest hearts and pierced souls like a knife!
When Jesus said "I came to call all sinners to repentance"
He spoke the truth regardless of the levels of acceptance.

You're not the first to hear His words and strongly disagree,
The opposition of *His* time nailed Him to a Tree!
When Jesus hung upon that Cross, the weight of sin to bear,
There was nothing "make-believe" about the reason He was there.

Christ died to save the human race, He died for me and you!
I'll share this message even if you don't believe it's true.
His sacrifice is where God's love and justice were displayed
And so there is no other name by which we must be saved!

No one else defeated death, no one paid for sin.
Every other "god" falls short, we have to look to *Him*!
The Man who walked through history and *proved* He was Divine,
Whose birth fulfilled the prophesies from which we measure time!

You see dear Mr Atheist, I too speak with conviction!
I know that Jesus loves you, this is fact and never fiction!
Look again dear friend to the God you have denied,
Does your disbelief or hatred *still* seem justified?

His mercy He extends to you with kindness and persistence;
Please don't mistake God's *patience* for "proof" of non existence.
He calls to every heart but should we choose to be obtuse,
When comes the day of judgement we will be without excuse.

I ask you Mr Atheist, please open up your mind.
Use the brilliant brain *He* gave you, truth is there to find!
I pray you'll come to know your God, your Saviour sacrificed.
God loves you Mr Atheist. Sincerely, yours in Christ.

SCRIPTURE REFERENCES

Deuteronomy 4:39; Proverbs 9:10; Psalm 14:1; Proverbs 12:16;
Judges 17:6; Romans 9:20; Romans 11:33-34; Job 40:1-14

REST IN PEACE

I wrote this poem especially for my Grandmother. After a long battle with Alzheimer's disease she was called home to be with her Saviour in September 2015.

During her ninety four years on Earth she made quite an impression on pretty much everyone who met her and my Gran could certainly be described as a lady ahead of her time! I wanted to write a poem that would express my gratitude for having been a part of her life but also my gratitude for our Saviour Jesus Christ. There never seems to be a time that more readily highlights the awesome power of the Cross than when we lose a loved one in the faith.

When I heard of my Gran's passing I felt a mixture of emotions all at once: relief that she was no longer suffering, sorrow at her absence and an overwhelming sense of gratitude and joy that she was now celebrating her first moments in eternity with Jesus.

When I try to picture what it must have felt like spending all those years slipping further and further into darkness and confusion, I can only imagine her sheer joy at waking up in Heaven to perfect clarity! I love to imagine her amazement at seeing the face of her Saviour and hearing His voice speak those blessèd words, "Welcome home, good and faithful servant." My heart overflows with gratitude when I picture this and I can't help but smile in spite of my own sorrow.

It's for this reason that my poem is called "Rest In Peace." This may seem like an obvious choice of title for an occasion such as this but the title does not in fact refer to my Gran because I know she's fine. She's more than fine! She's having the best time she's ever had!

The title instead refers to the peace that I rest in knowing that my Gran is now in the wonderful company of our Lord Jesus Christ. It refers to the peace that I rest in knowing that thanks to the awesome work Jesus did for us on the Cross, one day I will see my Gran again and it will be the beginning of our eternity together praising the one who made it all possible. To God be the glory forever and ever. Amen.

POEM

Dearest one, the winter is over
And the sun has finally set.
Though you leave me in sadness and sorrow,
In my heart I feel no regret.

I think through the years of my lifetime
And how you have always been there.
To imagine you no longer with us
Leaves a void oh so empty and bare.

As a baby you cradled and held me,
As a tot I was bounced on your knee.
The games that we played in my childhood
Are now just a fond memory.

I think of our countless adventures,
How we'd leave the real world behind
As we walked through fantastical forests!
We'd imagine such fun in our minds.

Years passed and we formed a deep friendship.
Times we shared in my heart I replay.
We'd sing about sweet bonnie Scotland
As we'd sit in the sunshine all day.

I'd listen to tales from your childhood,
How outrageous you were for your time!
I took joy in creating the picture
Of you in your youth and your prime.

In my thoughts I can visit these moments.
Special times that I'll always recall.
Re-live them and treasure them always
And feel grateful we shared them at all.

How blessed I feel to have known you.
You were grandmother, mother and wife.
Your existence imprinted within me,
Ever more you'll be part of my life.

But now I am here in the present
With the thought of your absence so stark.
I know that this pain won't consume me
For a light that is piercing the dark.

I remember you spoke of our Saviour,
Of the joy His salvation would bring.
Many times your peace was a witness
Of a life living under His wing.

Your words planted seeds in my spirit
And encouraged me not to let go.
Your faith was a gentle reminder
Of the Saviour *I* wanted to know.

For this I'm eternally grateful
Though you knew not the purpose you played.
The rewards you will reap now in Heaven
For your faith and the difference you made.

I know on this Earth I will miss you
And though tears of deep sorrow I'll weep,
Lamentations I'll turn into worship
For in Jesus you've fallen asleep.

He knew of the pain death would bring us
But His work on the Cross has sufficed.
He's abolished sin's claim on the captives!
So I rest in the promise of Christ.

When my days here on Earth are but over
And I walk through that heavenly door,
When it's *my* turn to meet with our Saviour,
I know I'll meet you too once more.

When I think of this gift Jesus gave us,
His love manifest through Son of Man,
Eternity won't seem sufficient
To express just how grateful I am.

For your arms once again they will hold me,
Your face once again I will see.
Forever we'll dance in God's glory!
So completed and perfect we'll be.

Though time made it's claim on your body,
The result of our fall took it's toll,
My heart is at peace with the knowledge
That death has no grip on your soul.

Before your days here were outnumbered,
Before it was time to depart
You acknowledged that Jesus is Saviour
And accepted Him into your heart.

So now you are dancing with Angels,
Reuniting with friends from your past.
Fulfilment I cannot imagine
And your joy will eternally last.

You'll rejoice in your heavenly body,
One that time cannot ravage or touch.
Eternally free from life's burdens;
Only Jesus can offer so much.

No more will you face trial or trouble,
No more you face sorrow or pain.
These things are not even a memory
And you'll think of them never again.

So I rest in the peace that you're happy,
I rest in this knowledge alone.
As you bask in the wonders of Jesus,
I rest in the peace that you're home.

SCRIPTURE REFERENCES

Psalm 116:15; Matthew 25:21; 1 Thessalonians 4:13-18;
Revelation 21:3-4

In The Shadow Of The Cross

Having reached the end of December 2015 I had been experiencing the joy of being surrounded by all the festive lights and nativity scenes. I'm a huge fan of Christmas time and all that it brings but one thing I had become very aware of was how romanticised the image of the birth of Christ has become.

The brutal reality of that cold night is replaced by warm, cozy stables, sweet looking animals and twinkling starry skies. I don't have an issue with this of course as I love a nativity scene but I began to reflect on how different the actual event must have been for all involved.

The thought of a desperate and frightened Mary giving birth in a gloomy stable while surrounded by stinking animal filth is quite a different picture. It's certainly not the ideal environment for a young mother to bring a baby into the world!

I think it may be partly due to the glamorised version we have that many people have no issue with a nativity scene but take huge issue when faced with the image of Jesus on the Cross. Clearly one is much more upsetting than the other for obvious reasons but there's certainly nothing threatening about the image of a Baby. The sight of a Man dying on a Cross on your behalf however is a much more challenging picture to embrace. These two images are inseparable though because the Baby in the manger is the same Person as the Man on the Cross; the nativity scene is simply the prelude to the Crucifixion and Resurrection scenes.

It was this that got me thinking about how the Cross was always the pivotal part of the story when it comes to the Baby in the manger. Knowing why Christ had come and how He knew His whole life was leading up to the pre-eminent moment when He would be crucified for the sins of the world, I suddenly couldn't see any stage of Jesus' life without it being overshadowed by the shape of the Roman Cross.

It was this thought that inspired me to start writing my poem and my hope is not to take away from the beautiful atmosphere of the time when we celebrate the birth of Christ. Rather it's to simply tell a more detailed story about this amazing Man and perhaps create a fuller picture of who the incredible Baby in the manger is.

POEM

In the shadow of the Cross a woman is chosen,
Deemed to be worthy and part of God's plan.
Placed in her womb as Heaven is opened,
The moment in time when God became Man.

In the shadow of the Cross lies a Babe in a manger,
A fragile gift from Heaven above.
A Child born to die and become a great Saviour,
His sacrifice found in the heart of true love.

In the shadow of the Cross three gifts are presented:
Frankincense, myrrh and the finest of gold.
Each with deep meaning, His life represented;
Their purpose prophetic and soon to unfold.

A gift to acknowledge His heritage Royal;
A metal so precious and brought from the East.
Myrrh for His death, to embalm Him in oil
While Frankincense spoke of our Greatest High Priest.

In the shadow of the Cross there lies a new mother,
Reduced by the pain and exhaustion of birth.
Contently she cradles this Babe like no other;
The Saviour of all and God of the Earth.

In the shadow of the Cross there sits a young Jesus,
Keenly He listens and learns of God's ways.
Astonishing all of the temple's great teachers,
Knowing the purpose and point of His days.

Greatly aware of His Heavenly mission,
Placed on the Earth to suffer great loss.
Pleasing the Father fulfilling His vision;
Saving mankind with His death on the Cross.

Deep in that shadow the Saviour is tempted,
Led in the wilderness forty long days.
Showing the devil his reign will be ended
And man once again will give God his praise!

In the shadow of the Cross Christ prays in the garden,
Knowing His hour is now drawing near.
Taking the blame and seeking our pardon,
Resolving to die for His children so dear.

Enveloped in darkness the King is arrested,
Tortured and beaten to save you and me.
Placed on His shoulders, each fibre invested,
Engulfed by it's shadow, Christ carries the Tree.

In the shadow of the Cross His mother kneels weeping,
Helplessly watching her suffering Son.
Bearing the stripes that would bring others healing,
Knowing that *this* was the *reason* He'd come.

Strong to the end, our Saviour succeeded!
Conquering death to make a new way.
Rising again, His work is completed.
Glory to God for there dawns a new day!

In the shadow of the Cross I stand here forgiven!
Thankful my heart could receive mercy's call.
Never forgetting the grace that I live in,
He's King of my heart and King over all!

Oh what a wonderful, mighty Redeemer!
Praise to our Saviour in whom we delight.
Thanks to the Babe who was placed in a manger,
Forever we'll dwell in His glorious light!

SCRIPTURE REFERENCES

Luke 1:26-33; Philippians 2:5-11; Revelation 1:17-18

INCORRUPTIBLE BEAUTY

INSPIRATION

This poem was inspired by 1 Peter 3:3-5 which reads,

"Do not let your adornment be merely outward—arranging the hair, wearing gold, or putting on fine apparel—rather let it be the hidden person of the heart, with the incorruptible beauty of a gentle and quiet spirit, which is very precious in the sight of God."

These verses have always stood out to me and have raised several questions in my heart over the years. I think it's an easily agreeable concept when Peter talks about placing more value on the inner character of a woman than what she looks like on the outside but I think the challenge for me comes when he talks about women having a "gentle and quiet spirit."

What's interesting is I've discovered over time that I'm not alone in my quandaries and it would seem that some other women find these verses quite hard to relate to as well. At times I've heard ladies comment on this section, frequently with an air of confusion and sometimes slight unease. I remember once hearing a lady say, "We're encouraged to have a "gentle and quiet spirit" but what does that even mean?"

Of course we have to take these words into context and we can see from the verses just before that Peter is addressing married women. He's encouraging them to conduct themselves in a certain manner in order to be a godly witness to a non-believing or unruly husband. Even within this framework though I think these words are still quite thought-provoking and it made me really wonder, what is it about this Scripture that makes it so challenging to embrace? Not for every woman of course but it does seem to stand out to quite a few!

I began to pray about it and ask the Lord for guidance and wisdom, knowing it was important for me to have a biblical understanding about the meaning expressed in this verse. After all, God's Word is perfect. It's the same yesterday, today and forever and the truths within are just as applicable to us today as they were to the people when they were first written.

I then found myself thinking about the contrast Peter makes between outer and inner beauty. When we think of "beauty" it's so easy to instantly think of the outer appearance. Often as people we spend ample time working on what we look like on the outside but if we're honest with ourselves, would we find that we pour the same levels of energy into what the inner person looks like? Most people would admit to consulting a mirror every day to ensure that the "outer person" is up to scratch but do we consult our Bibles just as often to make sure the "inner person" is looking good?

This inspired me to start writing the first few verses of my poem and as I continued to write I realised that it wasn't just with the focus of being a married woman but also as a Christian woman living in a very anti-Christian world. Before long I felt the Lord ministering to my heart and it's this open and honest process that I share through my poem "Incorruptible Beauty."

POEM

Mirror mirror on the wall, tell me what you see.
In silence you reflect the form my Maker gave to me.
The image that I know so well and tend to every day
Submits to subtle change as time ticks steadily away.

You watch me with indifference as I comb and style my hair.
You never give opinions on the jewellery that I wear
And though you've never commented on how my clothes have changed,
I find I must consult you as each outfit is arranged.

You show me with such honesty the lines my face accrues;
At times the truths that you reveal aren't always what I'd choose!
But you are always faithful to display what needs attention.
I find I'm rather grateful for your timely intervention!

But mirror mirror on the wall, sometimes I may hide
What's *really* going on deep down and what I feel inside.
The image I present to you will show no hint of strife
Though maybe you might catch a glimpse of pressures in my life.

But mirror mirror don't you see although you play your part,
You don't reveal my spirit or condition of my heart.
You needn't get upset for though reflection *is* your goal,
You can't expose or replicate the colour of my soul.

The picture you provide can go no deeper than my skin,
You don't possess authority to show me what's within.
So though your eyes are limited and only see so far
You really needn't fuss or fret, it's just the way things are.

For if your eyes *could* see my soul I'd think it quite absurd!
To view my *true* reflection I must look within God's Word.
It's here I learn my Maker sees the heart He made by hand,
Whose eyes cannot be fooled and where no trickery can stand.

Although this thought is daunting and a challenge to embrace
It's also liberating for I'm covered by His grace.
To stand before my Father and consult His thoughts above
I know the truths that *He* reveals are driven by His love.

So though I face some ugly traits that beg for circumvention
I find I'm rather grateful for *His* timely intervention!
He gently shows me where my heart might need a nip or tuck
And with each revelation deepest habits come unstuck.

And so instead of worrying about my double chin
The flaws I need to focus on are those that lie within!
So as I delve within His Word they're dealt with one by one
And all the time He's moulding me to look more like His Son.

To look like Him in *character* is such a worthy aim!
To have my life reflect His soul and honour Jesus' name.
Oh but what a challenge of the very highest grade!
A mission quite impossible if not for Jesus' aid.

He sends the Holy Spirit who instructs me every day,
Who teaches me in simple truth and guides me in His way.
Who shows me God's great love for me in spite of every flaw!
Who helps me understand His Word and fills my heart with awe.

Awe for such a masterpiece! A perfect work of art!
Inspired Holy Scriptures that speak straight into my heart.
I've found there is no other book that makes my spirit soar,
Such power that can build me up yet cut me to the core!

It isn't just my sinful flesh that wars within this vessel,
God's Word can be so challenging and cause my soul to wrestle!
For every page reveals to me the heart of the Divine
And so *my* heart is scrutinised to make sure it's in line.

So when it comes to Peter and his words in chapter three,
I find that his description is quite curious to me.
I read about some qualities that bring my God delight,
"A gentle, quiet spirit" is what's precious in His sight.

These interesting adjectives stand out upon the page,
These words don't seem to tally with this modern day and age.
A message much more popular is "stand out from the crowd!"
"Make sure you're voice is always heard, be brassy, bold and loud!"

"Be unapologetic in how brazen you might be.
Declare "Because I'm worth it!" Make it clear for all to see!"
Of course this stance is secular and not what I would choose.
This certainly does not reflect my feelings, thoughts or views.

And yet I find I'm searching for the meaning that's asserted,
Does Peter mean that women *can't* be fun and extroverted?
What if she's outgoing and expressive in her ways?
Will she be displeasing to her Saviour all her days?

Will natural vivacity be looked upon as "sin?"
Are these words to "silence" us and box all women in?
This thought is not affirming for the female self esteem;
I question if these words are as restrictive as they seem.

To subjugate all women would be quite an implication.
Merely the suggestion leads to insubordination!
So either I'm mistaken or I just don't understand,
This concept and the God *I know* do not go hand in hand.

For Jesus doesn't box us in or make us all the same,
He blesses us with different traits to glorify His name.
Variety is what reveals the skill of our Creator,
He's Saviour of our souls and women's greatest Liberator.

So keeping this in mind I lift these verses up in prayer
And ask the Holy Spirit to reveal the meaning there.
I firstly question "gentle" and the qualities it brings,
I wonder what I'd look like if I *don't* apply these things?

The opposite of "gentle" is described as rough or rude,
A character that's uncontrolled, unfriendly, coarse and crude.
It's also disagreeable, uncivil and severe,
It's merciless and unrefined and grating to the ear.

It's violent and it's hateful where no self control may rule.
It's known for being impolite and callous, harsh and cruel.
To read this unappealing list it really does appall,
These aren't the kind of traits I want to see in me at all!

The opposite of "quiet" is described as being loud,
A character that's thunderous and vulgar, brash and proud.
It's forceful and it's mouthy with a blaring quality.
Oh God forbid my friends should find these attributes in me!

These negative descriptions don't reflect my God Divine
And I don't look for these in those with whom I spend *my* time.
So if I don't appreciate these traits when found in others
Then why should I inflict these on my sisters and my brothers?

A spirit that *is* "gentle" is courteous and calm
With tender hearted ways which can be soothing like a balm.
It's temper is controlled when faced with heated opposition,
It's genial and loving with a kindly disposition.

It's pleasant and considerate, refined and affable,
Compassionate and disciplined and also merciful.
This lovely, warm description speaks of traits I'd like to show.
It's also fair to note it sounds just like a *Man* I know.

A spirit that is "quiet" would be cool and undisturbed.
Described as unassuming, discreet and unperturbed.
It's modest and it's stable, it's collected and serene.
It's still and unobtrusive, avoiding the obscene.

A quiet spirit gives no trouble willingly to any.
The traits I find desirable within *this* list are many!
This explanation pulls me in with every definition,
The fact I want to *know* this person asks for recognition.

Suddenly the adjectives I thought were unappealing
Speak to me directly and provoke a different feeling.
I know that my initial thoughts are truly sacrificed
For all of the above are things I see displayed in Christ!

The toughest *Man* in history whose *strength* endured the Cross
Displayed the *gentlest* traits this world has ever come across!
The God whose power formed the Earth and all the Heavenly host
Lived the kind of life I'd like to emulate the most.

And so to look at Peter's words it's very clear to see,
A "gentle, quiet spirit" is what I wish to be!
No longer do I struggle to apply these to myself
For Jesus doesn't ask for things He didn't do Himself.

He set the best example of humility and love,
Always coinciding with His Father's will above.
He sought the undesirable, embraced the ostracised
Yet always spoke in love and truth and never compromised.

He demonstrated perfectly His grace and self control
Yet boldly spoke to hypocrites and pierced their very soul!
The God who could rebuke the waves and rein a demon in
Humbly knelt to wash the feet of those who followed Him!

His life so full of paradox and stunning contradiction;
With *power over all* He came to *serve* with such conviction!
He shattered preconceptions as the humble, servant King.
It's clear His words have been profound whatever year they're in!

Christ's influence on Earth cannot be said to be a myst'ry
When this gentle, quiet Spirit, changed the course of hist'ry!
His Gospel message saw the start of women's liberation,
Cutting through the culture to proclaim emancipation!

The prejudice that women faced, His teachings would dispel.
His passion for equality led Him to a well.
Ignoring "current" views and seeking those of poor renown,
His disregard for gender turned opinions upside down!

The God who revolutionised the outlook of mankind
Left *all* discrimination and unfairness far behind.
So studying these Scriptures there's a truth I must recall;
Christ died for men *and* women and He paid the price for all!

Repressing womankind is clearly not the Bible's aim,
The picture is for all who want to glorify God's name.
The Holy Scriptures show us how to live in one accord,
We'd *all* do well to follow in the footsteps of our Lord!

To contradict *our* times and have Him reign within our heart
That really *is* a statement and will set our lives apart!
To truly make a mark in life and go against the grain,
I'll use my voice to boldly boast in only Jesus' name!

So Peter's words of guidance have a meaning I now see;
The most appealing ornaments are proof of Christ in me.
This beauty isn't made of gold or hanging from a chain,
It isn't set in silver with a posh designer name.

It's not a row of diamonds on a polished platinum ring,
This beauty shines the brightest when my soul reflects my King.
So though the lines of youthful splendour gently fade away,
Let's pray our *inner* beauty may grow brighter every day!

So Holy Bible in my hands, tell me what you see.
With power you reflect the soul my Maker gave to me.
May beauty incorruptible gain the greatest prize.
In Heaven we can shine because we're worth it in *His* eyes!

SCRIPTURE REFERENCES

Proverbs 31:30; 1 Timothy 4:7-8; 2 Corinthians 4:16;
Ephesians 5:25-28; Isaiah 40:8; Psalm 119:60; 2 Peter 1:19-20

HEAVEN'S SPLENDOUR

INSPIRATION

One day I was thinking about some of the descriptions the Bible gives us of what wondrous things await the Christian in Heaven. I was trying to picture how incredible it will be and began to wonder if anything in particular can possibly stand out as the most splendid thing in amidst so much beauty. It was this simple thought that inspired me to start writing "Heaven's Splendour."

My hope for this poem is that it can be a comfort and encouragement to us, especially in the midst of this time full of so much global unrest, violence and strife. My prayer is that it can be a wonderful reminder for us as Christians to keep our eyes looking upward, to focus on the eternal picture and know that there are unimaginable wonders awaiting us in Heaven.

POEM

To picture waking up in Heaven, mortal flesh redeemed at last!
Glistening streets of gold before me, pain and sorrow in the past.
What wondrous scenes and sights await me? Endless marvels to behold.
Things no earthly eye could fathom, awe no earthly heart could hold.

Stepping into life eternal, drinking in the beauty bright.
In amidst such stunning splendour what will be the *finest* sight?
Will it be the hosts of Heaven? Angels in their dwelling place!
Seeing mighty Gabriel or fearsome Michael face to face.

Will it be a splendid vision setting eyes on Abraham?
Seeing faithful Job before me, meeting God's most patient man.
Finding I'm among Apostles! Those who wrote the Scriptures true.
Standing with God's loyal servants, what a truly sterling view!

A stirring sight I know awaits me, one to steal my breath away;
Faces from my earthly life whose countenances shine like day.
Loved ones who have gone before me, I will see them once again!
How my heart will overflow to feel their arms embrace my frame.

Oh the blessèd treasures waiting, waiting there for me to see!
Dwelling in my Father's House, in paradise I'll surely be.
Numbered with the many brethren, voices raised in one accord;
Saints from all of history praising Jesus Christ our Lord!

What a task to try and picture multitudes with hands held high,
Witnessing a sea of souls united in their joyful cry!
Singing songs of adoration, sullied not by stains of sin.
Countless monuments of mercy come to worship Christ their King!

Oh to see the seated Saviour radiant upon His Throne,
Surrounded by eternal worship praising Jesus' name alone.
Who could comprehend such beauty? Who could grasp this wondrous
sight?
Seeing every soul redeemed now bathing in the Saviour's light!

Yet in the midst of all this splendour, all these precious sights to see
None will be *more* splendid than the scars my Saviour bears for me.
They'll speak of my unworthiness for Heaven cannot harbour pride;
Payment for my presence there displayed on hands and feet and side.

What love is this? Sing Hallelujah! Blessèd be His mighty name!
Jesus Christ, my soul's Redeemer took my sin and hid my shame!
Proof of love beyond all measure, scars in which I'll boldly boast.
My worth imprinted in His palms, *this* sight is what I'll value most.

Heaven's only man-made vision saves me from a darker fate.
I *would* shed tears of gratitude but there are no tears past the Gate.
Instead I'll shout with joyous praise! For all eternity I'll sing,
"Glory, glory! God Almighty! Thou art worthy, Christ my King!"

Oh to see the eyes of Jesus! Oh to hear Him gently say,
"Such is my great love for you I paid to wash your sins away."
How I'll kiss those hands of Jesus! Kiss the scars He bears for me,
With truth to claim forevermore, *all* Heaven's splendour found in Thee!

SCRIPTURE REFERENCES

Isaiah 49:16; 1 Corinthians 2:9; Psalm 44:8

A Higher Calling

It would seem that the year 2016 was a very interesting one for politics and global unrest. As a result I began to see many heated debates and extremely ugly arguments appearing on social media, sometimes even amongst Christians. It was this that inspired me to write my poem.

My prayer is that the poem can encourage us all to pray for our leaders just like the Bible exhorts us to do in 2 Timothy 2:1-2 where it says,

"Therefore I exhort first of all that supplications, prayers, intercessions, and giving of thanks be made for all men, for kings and all who are in authority, that we may lead a quiet and peaceable life in all godliness and reverence."

I also hope it can encourage us to keep our eyes on Jesus regardless of what our own political persuasions might be. As Psalm 133:1 says,

"Behold, how good and how pleasant it is for brethren to dwell together in unity!"

Poem

Brethren, do not fret and quarrel. Do not wallow in despair.
Keep your focus Heaven bound and find your peace in humble prayer.
Take your rest in Holy Scriptures, do not war within your soul.
Always keep in mind the truth that Jesus Christ *is* in control.

Let's not give our hearts to worry or the sorrow it can bring;
Striving with those close to us as if we do not know our King!
Never find us pointing fingers, cursing others to our shame.
If we *must* succumb to pointing let us point to Jesus' name!

We don't look to man or woman, putting hope in empty words,
Knowing that their promises will fly away like startled birds.
Ours is such a higher calling! Trusting in our God above,
Holding close *His* promises while showing all Agape love.

Though our views may often differ, let disputes and squabbles cease.
Unified through Christ we'll stand as we aim to dwell in peace.
Let us not *neglect* our leaders, may we lift them up in prayer.
Ask that God would grant them wisdom, knowing *Christ* has put
them there.

No one gains their earthly power by the will of man alone;
All of their authority is granted by God's sovereign Throne.
Whether we support their vision, whether we give vain applaud,
Let us rest in knowing they're appointed by the hand of God.

Given place to serve *His* purpose, His objectives to fulfil.
Nothing will unfold that's not according to His sovereign will.
Let's submit to Jesus' wisdom knowing He is fair and just.
Certain in *His* character, in *Christ* we safely place our trust.

Nothing can surprise our Saviour, nothing goes against His plan.
He is one who *keeps* His word and holds us in His mighty palm.
He has said He'll never leave us, never let us drown in fear,
Vowing He will meet our needs and wipe away our every tear.

Promising in times of darkness He will give us strength to cope,
Thinking of our future days with thoughts of peace to give us hope.
May we look to Christ our Shepherd as He leads us with His staff.
Let's give God His rightful place and let Him work on our behalf!

Brothers do not be despondent, sisters do not be enticed.
Turning neither right nor left, we're centred in the truth of Christ.
Brethren let us not be sleeping, we are in the final days!
Rise above the petty scoffing, shun profane and idle ways!

Scriptures tell us Christ is coming! All *will* bow down at His feet;
Ruling over Washington and making naught of Downing Street.
Dwelling in these latter days our unity we must preserve.
Yes we vote for leaders here but let's remember *who we serve!*

Jesus Christ, the God of Heaven! Lord and Ruler over all!
At a single word from Him all the earthly kingdoms fall!
Let us not forget His power! God forbid we vainly grope.
Let us not behave as if we've lost our faith and have no hope!

We have such a higher calling! Looking to our perfect Guide,
Watchful as the stage is set, He's coming back to claim His Bride!
Though we live in times of peril God is *still* upon His Throne.
May we lift our eyes to Heaven knowing Christ will lead us home!

SCRIPTURE REFERENCES

Romans 13:1-2; 2 Timothy 2:23-3:5; Jeremiah 29:11; Proverbs 4:27;
Proverbs 16:20

THE BURDEN OF WAITING

INSPIRATION

I've been learning over the last few years that some trials are like the seasons we have with the weather and last for a relatively short time. There are other trials however that don't seem to come to a close after what we would class as a "season" and continue to rumble on and on.

When weeks turn into months and months turn into years it can be such a challenge not to become completely disheartened. When family and friends are longing to hear of an improvement in your situation and yet all you have to tell them is that nothing has changed and you're still just waiting on the Lord and trusting in Him, it can be very difficult and frustrating for both sides. For some people years can even turn into decades and they still find themselves praying for their loved one to be saved or for the physical or financial trials to ease.

Of course there are varying kinds of storms that we go through in life and I think it's important to know the difference between a storm of correction and a storm of instruction.

If we've been rebellious or disobedient in our walk with the Lord, perhaps living in a manner that we know is contradictory to the Word of God then it's certain that we'll find ourselves in the midst of a time of correction. If we're truly born-again and not just "Christian" by title then living in disobedience to God will grieve the Holy Spirit and convict us in our hearts. God loves us and like any good, loving father would do with a wayward son or daughter, He'll bring us into a time of chastening to bring us back into line with His Word and His will. It's not a mean-spirited thing to do, it's the loving protection of a God who wants and knows what's best for us. It may be painful for a time but ultimately we'll thank Him as He seeks to restore our fellowship with Him.

The inspiration for this poem however comes not from going through a storm of correction but rather one of instruction. I'm talking about the kind of trial you find yourself in even though you know you've been following Jesus the whole time and this is the place God has brought you to. A storm of instruction is very different in nature because it has nothing to do with disobedience.

If we consider the fact that Jesus was in the centre of God's will when He hung on the Cross, it certainly goes against the suggestion that anyone going through a painful time of trial must be rebelling or backslidden. The book of Job in the Bible tells us about all the awful trials he went through as a servant of God and yet he was described as a "blameless and upright" man in Job 1:1.

In Mark 4 we read about Jesus and His Disciples during a storm that was so ferocious it would seem it was demonically driven. Jesus commanded the storm "Quiet! Be still!" but in the original Greek text His words translate as "Be muzzled" or "Be gagged."

We too can be exactly where God wants us to be and yet find ourselves battling with storms so terrifying we wonder if we're going to make it. Not all trials in life are there because of a sin issue, some come our way because God wants us to learn something about Him that only this situation can teach us. Sometimes we can find ourselves right in the middle of a storm at the same time as being right in the centre of God's will.

It was during such a time as this when I found myself reading Psalm 13 which says,

"How long, O Lord? Will You forget me forever?
How long will You hide Your face from me?

How long shall I take counsel in my soul,
Having sorrow in my heart daily?
How long will my enemy be exalted over me?

Consider and hear me, O Lord my God;
Enlighten my eyes,
Lest I sleep the sleep of death;

Lest my enemy say,
'I have prevailed against him';
Lest those who trouble me rejoice when I am moved.

But I have trusted in Your mercy;
My heart shall rejoice in Your salvation.

I will sing to the Lord,
Because He has dealt bountifully with me."

The first line really stood out to me and I felt I could relate to David's cry of despair. Although as Christians we know that God has promised to never leave or forsake us as Hebrews 13:5 says, I think there are times in life when it can feel as if God has perhaps forgotten us. This is of course never the case as even when we can't feel God's presence He is always there and He's always working on our behalf. God doesn't break His promises and it's often in these times of drought that He's doing things behind the scenes in an incredible way!

It's encouraging though to hear in this Psalm that even King David, the man after God's own heart also went through trials like these. I was amazed that after such a dramatic opening to the Psalm, by the fifth verse David's tone changes and he's quickly back to focusing on God's goodness. I found this journey from despair to trust really encouraging and inspiring and so began to write my poem "The Burden Of Waiting."

The title comes from the feeling that going through a long trial can seem like just waiting for things to change has become the burden that you have to carry through each day. A heavy burden is of course never from Jesus though as He says in Matthew 11:29-30,

"Take My yoke upon you and learn from Me, for I am gentle
and lowly in heart, and you will find rest for your souls. For My
yoke is easy and My burden is light."

My prayer for this poem is that it can encourage anyone who feels like they're going through an on-going trial. The devil would have you believe it's your fault and that you're alone in the situation. You're not!

Many are going through similar difficulties and you're in good company! Jesus is with you, His grace is sufficient for each day and He will get you through this. Just keep trusting in His wisdom and sovereignty and don't give up hope. We only hope in things we can't see otherwise it's not hope so even if things look bleak, keep hoping! Your Saviour is with you, He loves you and He will give you the strength you need in this time.

POEM

How long, O Lord? Will You forget me forever?
How long must I wait in this troublesome place?
Consider and hear me, enlighten my vision.
Remember Your servant and hide not Your face.

How long must my soul take counsel within me?
How long must I carry this sorrow of heart?
Though seasons may change *this* season seems endless.
How long must I wait Lord to see a new start?

Yet better it is to trust in Your mercy
Than groping for answers I won't understand.
Instead of requests and demands in the darkness
Much better it is Lord to reach for Your hand.

What could be wiser than following Jesus
Though others may deem it brings little reward?
When all of their questions will meet the same answer
And all I can say is "I wait on the Lord."

Help me to carry this burden of waiting,
Let not my spirit seem lost and forlorn.
Help me to offer my praise in the desert,
Recalling Your love in the eye of the storm.

For not every trial is filled with a clamour,
Though "quiet" and "warfare" seem strangely opposed.
Sometimes the challenge is filling the silence
When once doors were open but now remain closed.

Days that *were* busy instead become aimless,
Heavenly gifts are put back in their box.
Reduced to "observer" as others continue
While years seem to pass with the ticking of clocks.

Hearing the devilish whispers of Satan
Filling the head with such worry and doubt.
Groping for Jesus amidst the confusion,
That flicker of Light that never goes out.

I know that Your presence is faithfully with me
And You have not given a spirit of fear
But one of sound mind, of love and of power!
I cry out to You Lord and know that You hear.

Help me to patiently wait for Your timing,
Refining my faith as I hope in Your Word
For time and again it's truth has been proven!
Make me a witness so hearts may be stirred!

Days are *not* aimless when focused on You Lord,
Serving Your purpose my skills are refined.
This training prepares me for what's round the corner;
My gifts are not boxed, they're just paused for a time.

Or maybe You're teaching me lessons anew Lord,
Developing skills that are yet to unfold.
Though various trials may grieve and perplex me,
A genuine faith is more precious than gold!

I trust in Your wisdom, You guard and protect me.
My soul, don't despise the day of small things!
Wherever I go may I represent You Lord
And seize every moment this circumstance brings.

Help me to see You in each situation,
Let naught be done through the arm of the flesh.
The work You've begun *will* be brought to completion
So fill me each day with Your Spirit afresh!

My mouth will continually praise and exalt You,
Your goodness and mercy I'll boldly proclaim!
Humbly I give back this life that You purchased;
My worth found in You, I rejoice in Your name!

The joy of the Lord is my strength and my comfort,
I cling to each promise when doubts pose a threat.
I know You'll establish the work of my hands Lord
For You are my God and You never forget.

When I think of Your heavens, the work of Your fingers,
The moon and the stars which You have ordained
What *is my life* that You should be mindful?
Oh Jesus, how faithful to me You've remained!

So help me to count it all joy in this trial.
Teach me, my Father to number my days.
Knowing I wait in Your arms everlasting,
I'll come out victorious and give You the praise!

Scripture References

Psalm 27:13-14; Psalm 61:1-2; 1 Peter 1:6-9; Romans 5:1-4;
Romans 8:24-25; Deuteronomy 8:2; 2 Timothy 1:12

THE RACE

I was having a conversation one day with a group of people who were a mix of Christians and non Christians. We were discussing the rather sobering subject of sin and judgement and one man's comment really stood out to me. He was looking into Christianity at the time and as he was listening to what others were saying on the topic he decided to speak up and share his thoughts. He said,

"I totally get that people like Hitler and other murderers deserve judgement, I understand that. I agree that rapists, pedophiles and people who do awful things absolutely deserve to be judged, but my issue is when I hear that ordinary people like me are going to be judged too. I don't think I deserve judgement because I'm not a bad person." I really appreciated the young man's honesty and felt I could relate to his issue because I remembered saying something very similar myself before I gave my life to Jesus. I began to share an analogy with the group that I hoped would help shed some light on the Biblical view of "good and bad people" and what the standard is for going to Heaven when we die. A couple of months later I felt the Lord putting it on my heart to turn this analogy into a poem and found myself writing "The Race."

Something else that I felt was very important to share with the group that day and also with anyone reading this poem is that God loves us and wishes that none should perish. As the Bible says in 2 Peter 3:9,

"The Lord is not slack concerning His promise, as some count slackness, but is long-suffering toward us, not willing that any should perish but that all should come to repentance."

God wants us to be in Heaven with Him in eternity, it's why He sent His Son Jesus to die on the Cross to pay for our sins.

There are so many angles for discussion when it comes to sin and judgement and too many for me to go into here! My hope is that this poem might help us as we take on the challenging task of looking at ourselves truthfully in relation to sin and get us thinking about what it is Jesus has achieved for us through His death and Resurrection.

POEM

Such wonderful weather! A jolly fine day!
Soon the excitement would get underway.
A marvellous challenge across wind and sea.
Competitors numbering one, two and three.

Each was attempting to swim every mile
And so they embarked on their watery trial!
"Aim for the prize!" was the thought to embrace.
"Bang!" went the gun and so off went the race!

Forwards they dashed with a call to be brave
As each of them dove through the very first wave.
With cheers from the seashore starting to dim,
Disaster arose only two miles in!

"Alas! It goes badly!" the first swimmer cried.
"Just double your efforts!" the second replied.
But sadly he couldn't, his muscles were spent
So down to the depths the first swimmer went.

The second and third journeyed on at a rate,
Quite unaware of the first fellow's fate!
Onwards they traveled when just up ahead
They noticed a flag in a bold shade of red.

Their hearts filled with glee as they cut through the spray;
The ten mile marker! They'd made it half way!
But just as their strokes passed the little red flag
The second discovered he'd started to lag.

"Alas! It goes badly!" the swimmer cried out.
"Just swim!" cried the third "For there's no room for doubt!"
But his limbs were too weary, his joints had grown tight.
He dipped from the surface and sank out of sight.

On went the third with such gusto and strength,
He felt quite assured he could swim any length!
The sight that awaited him filled him with joy
For on the horizon he glimpsed land ahoy!

Steadfast he swam through the foam and the fizz,
Sure that the victory soon would be his!
But though his attempt had been really quite cracking
He suddenly found that his vigour was lacking!

Alas, it went badly so close to the mark!
He'd thought that he'd knock the ball clear out the park!
The race had been lost in spite of his wishes
So down went the third one to sleep with the fishes.

A sorrowful ending, it beggars belief!
None would have thought they could come to such grief.
So as our competitors meet with their end
Let's look at the moral together dear friend.

One did quite badly, the second okay,
The third was an inch from the end you could say!
One awful, one average, one glowing report!
But all three performances sadly fell short.

No trophy was lifted, no medal received.
The outcome was not what they would have believed!
Though efforts were varied the battle was lost,
All ended up paying the ultimate cost.

Achieving perfection they would have prevailed
But none could attain it so all of them failed.
A tale with a lesson for you and for me,
This troubling story has meaning you see.

We've gladly no part in this race full of strife
But how do we fare in the race we call "Life?"
Some are just evil and some are okay
While others are practically saints you might say!

We look to our deeds and achievements to gauge
How "good" or "bad" we'd be deemed in this age.
Although over time our failings may worsen,
Most of us claim that we're "not a bad person."

Stating our virtues, we couldn't be "gladder."
We'd probably place ourselves high up the ladder!
Judging our actions when next to our brothers
We measure ourselves by comparing to others.

We look down our noses though nobody should
And always find someone who makes us feel "good!"
Scorning our flaws which we'd rather excuse,
God must have heard every reason we use!

"*He* murdered millions and had affairs!
I've *never* fallen to such evil snares!
I can't believe I'll be judged for my sin.
Blameless I'm not but I'm better than *him*!"

"I don't really care what it says in God's Book,
The sins I've committed He'll just overlook!
I give to charity and feed the poor!
This claim that I'm "wicked" I cannot endure!"

But God doesn't judge us with balancing scales,
This incorrect view is the tallest of tales.
It seems that His law has been misunderstood,
Our wickedness can't be outweighed by our "good."

Though genuine kindness is pleasing to Him,
No one's "good deeds" can cover their sin.
This is a thought that needs some correction,
All come up short for the mark is *perfection*!

Works cannot save us, they will not suffice;
The standard is Jesus, the plumb line is Christ.
No one can claim to be empty of sin,
All of us fail when we stand next to Him!

His law is to show us that each is a sinner
But those found in Jesus come out as the winner!
It's why God invites us to open our eyes,
To trust in our Saviour and share in *His* prize!

No matter what glorious traits we've displayed,
The glory is His for by grace we are saved!
Though generous acts bring praise to God's Throne
Our hope and our faith are in Jesus alone.

Come, let us question and reason together;
Where are the ties that we really must sever?
Where is our confidence? Where is our boast?
What are the strengths we rely upon most?

Let us know *now* that to gain the reward,
We look to none other than Jesus our Lord!
Run with endurance to conquer life's race
And thanks to Christ Jesus we'll end in first place!

SCRIPTURE REFERENCES

Ephesians 2:8-9; Isaiah 64:6; Romans 3:10; Philippians 3:8-9;
Romans 3:20

Love Is...

Inspiration

There are many different opinions about "Love" these days and a countless variety of views on what love should look like. I often see things done under the banner of "Love" and yet they seem to have very little to do with it.

I felt inspired to write a poem based on what the Bible says about love because this incredible, prophetic Book tells us that God Himself is love (1 John 4:8) and that "All Scripture is given by inspiration of God..." (2 Timothy 3:16) I felt therefore that if there was one opinion worth listening to about what love is then it would be the opinion of the God who is the very source and embodiment of love!

I soon found myself writing the poem "Love Is..."

Poem

Love is patient, love is kind, love endures all things.
Love does not parade itself or boast in what it brings.
Love will never envy and love will not provoke,
It will not wear a false facade or hide behind a cloak.

Love will suffer long and not be quick to place the blame.
Love will seek to reconcile and overlook the shame.
Love is not debauchery expressed through wanton youth.
Love is pure and selfless and rejoices in the truth.

Delighting in the humble, setting arrogance aside,
Love is not puffed up and has no fellowship with pride.
Love is not a masquerade with mankind at it's worst.
Love will never seek it's own but put all others first.

It looks to be encouraging, affectionate and tender,
Love will not intimidate to force it's own agenda.
It won't insist that others *must* promote and *share* it's vision,
Love will always show respect when faced with opposition.

It finds no joy in wickedness or actions that are crude
But celebrates in righteousness for love is never rude.
It never thinks of evil in which there is no trust,
It won't embrace depravity, iniquity or lust.

It relishes in holiness and all that it entails,
Gratified through faithfulness for true love never fails.
Free from pompous piety, it reflects our Lord above.
Love will look like *godliness* because our God *is* love.

Echoes of *His* character should shine and shimmer through.
Love will not forsake the facts but point to what is true.
Love is our Creator when he said "Let there be light,"
Declaring all His hands had made was precious in His sight.

Love is God descending from His high and mighty Throne,
Coming in the form of flesh to seek and save His own.
Love is clearly seen upon our Saviour's bloodied face;
Love is Jesus on the Cross, dying in our place.

His sacrifice is where we see the Father's plan unveiled;
Triumphant over sin and death, Christ's love for us prevailed!
Rising from the grave, His Resurrection sets us free!
Our liberation bought through Him for all eternity.

Love is when our lives reflect our Saviour sacrificed
For love is all the colours of a soul redeemed by Christ.
Love is to acknowledge our Creator God above;
When *Jesus'* name is glorified then *that's* when love *is* love!

SCRIPTURE REFERENCES

1 John 3:16; 1 John 4:8; 2 John 1:6; 1 Corinthians 13:4-8; Romans 5:8

FIFTY YEARS

INSPIRATION

I wrote this poem especially for my Mother and Father in-law to help mark their Golden Wedding Anniversary. My hope is that the poem may be shared and used to bless other godly couples who are also celebrating this wonderful occasion!

POEM

Fifty years of marriage! Can you quite believe?
Fifty years of *happiness* not many can achieve.
Barely more than children when first you shared a gaze,
The moment when you saw the one with whom you'd spend your days.

Did either of you know this was your journey at the start
Or sense how much the other one would captivate your heart?
Fifty years together! A thought we must embrace.
Half a century and five decades of God's grace.

Think of all the laughter and the happy times you've seen.
Picture all the tender hugs and smiles there must have been.
Think of the adventures through the seasons of all weather,
Stronger in the trials as you faced the storms together.

Fifty years of teamwork and living as a pair.
Fifty years of selflessness and showing that you care.
Fifty years of partnership and walking side by side,
Your life a true example of our Saviour with His Bride.

Depths of love and faithfulness to which we all aspire,
A godly illustration and a marriage to admire.
Here's to many years to come so bless them Lord we pray.
We celebrate a golden couple on their golden day!

Scripture References

Song Of Solomon 2:16; Ephesians 5:25-29

A New Year's Prayer

Inspiration

In December 2017 I was on tour with the show "The Sound Of Music" and performing in Dublin, Ireland over Christmas and New Year. As New Year's Eve approached I found myself thinking over the year that had just passed and started to wonder what the months ahead would bring.

I'm not one for New Year's Resolutions but I did find myself thinking about what might be beneficial things to pray for when heading into a new year. I soon found myself writing a poem that I hope is easily relatable and that can be an encouragement when we look to the unknown future.

May fear and worry never dominate us and may we live instead in the life affirming fellowship with God made possible by the work of Jesus Christ. The only Man ever to enter Heaven through His own good works is able to keep what we have committed to Him until that Day. I pray this poem can inspire us all to draw ever closer to our Saviour, redeeming the time until His return!

Poem

Another year has reached it's end, the time is nearly through.
Reflecting on the months gone by I lift my hands to You
For when I view life's pages and the stories of my days
I see a book that's filled with grace and have to sing Your praise!

Remembering the times of joy when laughter came with ease,
It lifts my spirits still when I recall such days as these.
Of course there were the darker spells I couldn't understand
But even through the tears I was upheld by Your right hand.

Thank you for Your faithfulness, thank You for Your love.
Thank You for the blessings You have poured out from above.
Thank You for my family, for friendships old and new.
Thank you for Your Word that keeps me on the path that's true.

Thank You for sustaining me when trials seemed too great,
Thank You for Your wisdom when you told my soul to "wait."
I'm grateful that You listen and You share in all my cares.
Thank You for Your guidance and for answering my prayers.

You have been my constant Help, my Shelter and my Shield;
The heartache You have brought me through, the illnesses
You've healed.
How I sing Your praises Lord, my Light and my Salvation
Whether it be joyful song or quiet contemplation.

And so I stand before You as I look towards the new,
However many days I have I dedicate to You.
Write about Your goodness in the pages of my story,
Let others look upon my life and give *You* all the glory.

I pray for all Your people, that You'd set ablaze our hearts,
Surround us with Your mercy as another New Year starts.
Fill us with a hunger Lord to read Your Word each day,
May we know the fullness of Your love in every way.

Help us to redeem the time and may our days be spent
With tender hearts and spirits always willing to repent.
May we seek to serve with joy our sisters and our brothers,
Thinking less about ourselves and more on loving others.

I pray for Your protection Lord against the fiery darts,
Rid us of the idols on the altar of our hearts.
Align our soul's desires with the plans You have in store;
Remind us who our First Love is, the One whom we adore!

May our vision be refreshed, our thoughts revitalised.
Help us really contemplate our *value* in *Your* eyes.
Let us not be wearied by life's burdens or details,
Help us pray "Your will be done." The prayer that *never* fails!

We give to You our hopes and dreams and place them in Your care,
We put them in Your mighty hands and know they're safest there.
Help us speak of You and may we never be ashamed.
We pray a special prayer for those who suffer in Your name.

Grant us health and happiness and let our faith inspire
Those who've yet to know You and fulfil their heart's desire.
Help us guide the lost to You and draw them to Your side
For this could be the year when You come back to claim Your Bride!

And so we look ahead with faith, with hope our spirits burn.
May we bring You glory as we wait for Your return!
Fill us with the Holy Spirit's power once again.
All this we now commit to You. In Jesus' name, Amen.

Scripture References

Psalm 23:6; Ephesians 5:15-16; Psalm 27:1; Jeremiah 29:11;
Psalm 27:14; Psalm 32:7

What Did *You* Do?

Over the course of a few months I found myself working and travelling alongside some wonderful and talented people who happened to be non-believers. This meant I was given the opportunity on several occasions to share the Gospel with various different colleagues. After listening to life stories, differing issues and reasons why each individual didn't call themselves a Christian I found myself asking one particular question, "What are you going to do with Jesus?"

I went on to explain that we can have different viewpoints and opinions in life but the Person of Jesus Christ is a real, historical figure. It's a fact that this Man walked the face of the Earth over two thousand years ago, He claimed to be the Son of the living God and the only way to enter Heaven. My question to everyone was the same, "What are you going to do with this information?"

Sadly we know that every single one of us is going to die at some point, nobody gets out of here alive! No matter what we have chosen to believe in our lifetime there will come the moment when we come face to face with our Maker.

Now I adore talking about the love, grace, patience and mercy of God. It brings me so much joy to share with others how Jesus forgives everyone who comes to Him in repentance and it's His desire that none should perish. While I've found that delivering the message of grace is a relatively easy thing to do, the flip side to that however isn't quite as enjoyable. The message of death and judgement isn't a comfortable one to share but that doesn't make it any less important. I think it's imperative to give people the full picture so that they know what the options are.

The Bible tells us in Hebrews 9:27,

"It is appointed unto men once to die, but after this the judgement."

This may not be as popular as hearing about the grace and love of God but if I failed to deliver the full counsel of God then I would be derelict as a messenger of the Gospel of Jesus Christ. Yes God is a God of love but He's also a God of justice, judgement and wrath. To preach only God's love would be to give only one side of the coin and this would be a huge disservice to both the listener and the Gospel.

The word "Gospel" literally translates as "Good News." To receive the good news we must first understand the bad news which is that we are all sinners. As Romans 3:23 tells us,

"For all have sinned and fall short of the glory of God."

The Bible also tells us that sin must be punished. We read in Romans 6:23,

"For the wages of sin is death, but the gift of God is eternal life in Christ Jesus our Lord."

If sin didn't need to be punished then Jesus wouldn't have had to die on the Cross to pay for our sins. God's holy and righteous character means that He cannot have sin in His presence and so for us to dwell in Heaven with Him we must be cleansed of our sin.

Now some may argue "Well if God created us then He created the sin in us too!" This is incorrect as sin is not a created thing, sin is merely the absence of righteousness. To put it into material terms, if you were to see a hole in a wall you wouldn't claim the hole was a created thing in and of itself. It's not something you can pick up and take away. The hole is simply the absence of the brick that should be there. So it is with sin. Man was created to have perfect fellowship with God but when man rebelled against God then sin came into the world. Sin is the result of a lack of obedience.

We learn in Genesis 1:31,

"God saw all that he had made, and it was very good."

For God to look at all that He had made and see that it was good means that it did not include sin or death. These negative things came in after man's rebellion and so now we all are born with a sinful nature and live in a fallen world as a result. None of us would have behaved any differently in the Garden of Eden given the same choice as Adam and Eve. All of us have the free-will God has granted us and all of us have chosen to rebel against Him. I don't think anyone in their right mind would claim to be perfect and to have never sinned in their life.

The Bible clearly tells us in Romans 3:10,

"There is none righteous, no, not one."

Thankfully God's love for us meant that He didn't want us to remain trapped in our sin and so sent His Son Jesus to pay for our sins in our place. All of us are in need of our Saviour whether we like to admit to that or not and there is only one name given under Heaven by which we must be saved. Jesus Christ. He's the only One who paid for the sins of the world, including my sins and yours. The only way we can enter Heaven is to put our faith in Him and accept His gift of grace. No amount of "good works" will make up for the fact that we're sinful. Considering sin must be paid for with death, it will either be Christ's death on the Cross that covers us or it will be the death of our own souls in eternity. This is the last thing that God wants to happen but if this is what we choose by rejecting His Son Jesus then this is what we'll have decided for ourselves. This leads me back to the topic of judgement.

The truth is all of us will stand before God one day and we'll stand in one of two ways. We'll either stand in Christ, completely forgiven and fully cleansed from all of our sins and unrighteousness or we'll stand on our own, hoping that we can somehow persuade a holy, righteous God that we have a good case for our unbelief and rejection of His Son Jesus.

It's a fearful thing to fall into the hands of the living God and so my desire for people to know their loving Saviour inspires me to share this reality while there is still a chance for people to question their beliefs. Through these thoughts and experiences I found myself feeling inspired to write "What Did You Do?"

The poem begins with the picture of one who has just completed their time on Earth, they're now coming face to face with God the Father and hearing the questions their Maker may ask of them. The tone is in no way meant to be threatening but rather I've written it in the hope that the poem may act as a loving warning. My desire is that it may inspire someone to really question their rejection of Jesus Christ now while there is still time reconsider.

POEM

"What did you do with my Son called Jesus?
What did you make of His Heavenly claim?
Did you dwell on His words or dismiss Him as "fiction?"
Were your lips used to worship or slander His name?

What did you do with the grace He provided,
His death on the Cross that paid for your sin?
Did you look on His face and stare with indifference
Or did His death cause you to turn towards Him?

How did you use the time that I gave you,
The days I appointed to you from My Throne?
Did you willingly follow the ones who detest Me,
Blindly accepting *their* thoughts as your own?

Or were your eyes open to see My creation?
Did your heart ever question the Source of such wealth?
Blessed with free-will and a mind that could reason,
Did you use what I gave you and think for yourself?

What did you do with the Heavenly Scriptures,
My Letter of love to all of mankind?
Did you search for the truth laid bare in the pages
Or harden your heart and close up your mind?

Did you listen to those who brought you My Gospel?
How did your spirit respond to My call?
Were you found to be proud or willing and humble?
Did you ever accept that I'm Lord over all?

How did you use the skills that I gave you?
Were Heavenly gifts ever offered as praise?
Did you open your mind to seek your Creator
And let Me be Author and Lord of your days?

What did you do with My Son called Jesus?
Speak truthfully as you begin to recount.
The life that you led has met it's conclusion;
Your time has now come to give an account."

Oh what a sobering series of questions.
Questions we're better to ask ourselves now
While given the chance to look to our Saviour,
Respond to His love and willingly bow.

Bow in sheer awe to the mercy provided,
Feeling no dread when we come face to face.
Drenched in forgiveness, in love and compassion,
Fearing no judgement and saved by His grace!

How He desires that no one should perish,
Urging each soul to let go of their sin.
The Maker of all calls out to our spirits!
Receive God today and run towards Him!

Run to His goodness! Bask in His mercy!
Taste for yourself the sweetness He brings.
Dwell in His peace, be awed by His power,
Feel your heart praise Him and hear how it sings!

Allow me this moment to plead with your spirit,
I beg you to open your heart to His voice!
Please be aware, eternity beckons;
Where you will spend it comes down to *your* choice.

What did you do with God's Son called Jesus?
Will you be known when you come to the Gates?
Do not forsake the grace that's before you;
Today is the day, your salvation awaits!

Think on it now for how you will answer
When the eyes of the Lord are resting on you.
May you be clothed in the robes of the Saviour
When faced with the question, "What did *you* do?"

SCRIPTURE REFERENCES

John 14:6; Matthew 16:41-42; John 3:36; 1 John 5:12; John 5:24;
Romans 8:1; Philippians 2:4-11; Acts 20:27

RESURRECTION DAY

INSPIRATION

During the approach to Easter 2018 I was thinking about how Easter Sunday is the most important day in the Christian calendar. The first Easter Sunday was the day when the future of mankind was completely transformed by Jesus Christ through His Resurrection and His whole life had been leading up to this triumphant moment.

I suddenly found myself thinking about how it would be lovely to have a poem that rejoices in what He achieved for us and soon felt inspired to write "Resurrection Day."

POEM

Praise the Lord! Rejoice and sing! Not only is there joy in Spring!
May I be the first to say, "Happy Resurrection Day!"
Christ is Risen! This we know so let our praises overflow.
Worship Him who broke the chains, in Heaven He forever reigns!

Let's lift our hands in exaltation, giving thanks for our salvation.
Messiah's day at Calvary has won for us the victory!
Peace with God we *can* enjoy, let any tears be those of joy
For this is not a day for strife, rejoice in Christ who bought us life!

A miracle of God occurred and sin had not the final word!
The sting of death is gone at last, the brutal Cross is in the past.
Prepare your heart and make some room for Him who left an
empty tomb!
Our freedom Jesus Christ has won! Let's praise His name, the work
is done!

Oh Risen Saviour, Morning Star, we celebrate how great You are.
Let trumpets sound and voices sing, we praise our awesome
King of kings!
Lord have our hearts of admiration, hear these songs of adoration.
We honour You in every way, this joyous Resurrection Day!

SCRIPTURE REFERENCES

Matthew 28:1-10

Identity Crisis

Inspiration

During the Summer and Autumn of 2017 I found I suddenly had an influx of auditions coming in. I was learning so much material and adopting such a vast array of characters that I almost felt like I should be appearing on an episode of the program "Stars In Their Eyes!" The famous statement, "Tonight Matthew, I'm going to be…" wouldn't have seemed out of place at this point! I had been remarking to my husband one day in the midst of it all that it would be good to write a poem about all the different characters I was auditioning for. The idea remained just a thought for several months however as I went off on tour with a show not long after this.

When the tour finished and I returned to London a friend recommended I join a group which is a community of Christians within the creative industry. It consists of all different kinds of creative types from performers like myself to musicians, writers, directors, stage technicians and the like. It's a really great group of people who meet up every couple of weeks to chat over coffee, encourage one another and pray for each other's needs. In a tough city like London and a brutal industry like Performing Arts I think a group such as this is a wonderful connection to have. Talking with like-minded people and sharing in each other's successes and struggles can be so rewarding and refreshing.

It was during my first meeting with the group that one of the founders asked me if I had ever written a poem about being a Christian performer. I replied that sadly I hadn't but as I went home that day I started thinking about the idea that had taken root from all the auditions in 2017. I soon found myself feeling inspired to write "Identity Crisis."

Every anecdote that appears in this poem is genuinely something I've experienced as a performer and is meant to offer a humorous insight into the realities of the world of Performing Arts. I also hope and pray that it can really encourage other Christians, not only in my chosen industry but in any realm of life.

The challenges faced relating to identity, self-esteem, value and worth aren't exclusive to creative types, anyone can struggle with this. I hope these words can really point to the truth that Jesus never wants us to feel inadequate. I pray they can encourage us all to focus on our First Love and to know the sweetness of His presence and power as we walk in the glorious light of His love for us. This alone will bring us into the joy and fullness that only Jesus can bring into the human heart.

POEM

The life of a Performer, what wondrous joys there are,
Ranging from the fabulous to really quite bizarre!
To find yourself within a show, of course the main objection
While putting on your thickest skin to deal with the rejection!

But even when you've found success and been within a cast,
Unemployment always looms for contracts never last.
One week you're starring centre stage then find that all too soon
You're jumping through the hoops again in each audition room!

All comfort and security have met their bitter end,
You step up to the plate and need to prove yourself again.
I too have had to bid farewell to nightly acclamation
While bringing my portfolio back out of hibernation.

Dusting off my repertoire I look to the unknown
And pray I see my agent's name appear upon my phone!
With weeks of no auditions and my prospects looking grim,
I praise the Lord when suddenly they all come flooding in!

And so begins the challenge that all actors must endure;
Try your best to fit the bill no matter how obscure!
Before I know, I'm on my way, audition bag in hand
And pray my vocal chords achieve whatever notes they've planned!

Of course the first endurance test to face in my vocation
Is travelling on London tubes and *finding* the location!
With cancelled trains and bus detours, travel is a pain.
Ensuring I'm on time I get "the train before the train!"

Arriving with straight hair before the wind and rain could spoil it,
I shuffle to my "changing room," aka…the toilet.
Though some may think it glamorous and envy my career
The truth is, *every* job I've had has always started here!

And so I find I'm perched again upon a lidded seat
While placing loo-roll down to keep the germs off of my feet.
Assuming toilet bugs are over all that I can see,
I get "audition ready" and ignore my OCD.

They're looking for a Mezzo and a slight "Dickensian theme,"
So I exit from the toilet like an 1860's dream!
Before I know, it's time to shake off all my fear and doubt;
My name's been called so off I go to sing my poor heart out!

No time to think of how it went, I find I'm off again
This time it's for an advert and the break-down says "Look plain."
Forsaking all my lip gloss and ignoring facial shimmer
I head to the audition room without a hint of glitter.

Next day I have a vocal call so battle through a market
Then find to my alarm the room is lined with cushioned carpet!
Carpet, heels and nerves all soon combine to my dismay
As I realise acoustics will be absent for today!

Another break-down comes and so I travel through the city
And hope I've hit the balance of "nice face but not *too* pretty."
Next is "gym instructor, trim physique, who's #winning."
I rake through every drawer to get the top I find most slimming!

Next I'm told to learn a song and bring a "Rock Chick" status.
I start to rake through belts and clothes, this needs some apparatus!
Digging through my wardrobe for something not too raucous,
Concerned I'll delve so deep I'll end up meeting Mr Tumnus!

Back inside a toilet with another script and score
I'm pulling on my tights while trying not to touch the floor.
I slightly lose my balance so I grab the radiator,
Then come to the conclusion that I'll bleach that foot off later.

But if you want to know what makes me really come un-stuck,
It's every singer's fear, I wake to find my glands are up!
Doing all I can do to restore my dulcet tones,
I'm rescued by my steam pot and a box of vocal zones.

I'm up for understudy for "A woman passed her prime,
Who hasn't seen the light of day for really quite some time."
If *pastiness* is what they want I know I'll fit right in,
I'll scrub away the tan and utilise my Scottish skin!

I'm whiter than a ghost, "au naturel" is how I'll go.
No fake tan today, I'll blind them all with skin of snow!
But next I'm up for "Woman with exotic look" they say.
In quite the turnaround tonight I'll bathe in St Tropez!

Oh yes, Performing Arts can really leave you in a spin!
So many different parts to play and moulds you must fit in.
"Fifties' Icon," "Panto Fairy" then "Generic Mother."
I go with *one* identity emerging as *another*!

Memorising scores and scripts can set you in a whirl,
I change so many times I almost feel like Supergirl!
It doesn't seem to matter what shows I've done before,
Each time I must convince them I'm "The One" they're looking for!

The challenge of auditions is a mix of fear and hope,
A tricky act of balancing and walking a tight-rope!
But then there comes the moment that makes it worth it all,
The thing that every actor loves is when we get "The Call!"

The call to say the job is ours and we have won the part
And then begins the countdown to when rehearsals start!
But going through this process gives me cause for some reflection,
For value isn't based in man's acceptance or rejection.

At times I need reminding though this really *is* the case
For personal rejection is a brutal thing to face!
Bitter disappointment comes pursuing *any* dream
And leaves us feeling low and quite devoid of self-esteem.

Society will tell us that to be of any worth,
We must achieve some prominence or fame throughout the Earth.
Wealth and great possessions mean we're "shining like a star"
And levels of approval show how "valuable" we are.

But *healthy* self-esteem comes not from worldly acclamation,
It doesn't lie in man's applause or gushing admiration.
I realise my worth will not be found on my CV,
My self-esteem and value lie in **Jesus' love** for me.

The love that drove Him to the Cross to pay my debt in full!
The love that says my value supersedes the finest jewel.
The love that never wavers even when I know I'm failing.
The love I can rely upon, that's constant and unchanging.

Dwelling on these promises sets me free from strife,
My status as a child of God gives purpose to my life.
It's not about my talents or what *I* have achieved
But rather it's about the One in whom I have believed!

Focusing on Jesus means whatever my position,
I'm free to use my skills for *God* and not my own ambition!
Knowing my Creator is the Author of my story
Brings joy into my heart to know my days will bring *Him* glory!

This blesses me beyond compare and brings my spirit rest,
Confident my Saviour's plan is always what is best.
So even on the days so full of sorrow and oppression,
My soul finds peace in knowing I am *still* His prized possession.

A crisis of identity need never play a part;
The true and living God has put His stamp upon my heart!
To know that I am cherished brings me great security.
I'll aim to be the woman God intended me to be.

Seeking out His purposes for which I was designed,
Leaving insecurity and every doubt behind.
Safe within the knowledge that whatever job I'm in,
I know *exactly* who I am. I'm daughter of the King!

SCRIPTURE REFERENCES

Ephesians 2:10; Psalm 139:14; 1 John 3:1; 1 John 4:19; 1 Peter 2:9;
Romans 12:4-8; Matthew 11:28; Proverbs 3:5; Philippians 4:13

Wolf In Sheep's Clothing

Inspiration

This poem was inspired by Matthew 7:15-16 which reads,

"Beware of false prophets, who come to you in sheep's clothing, but inwardly they are ravenous wolves. You will know them by their fruits. Do men gather grapes from thorn-bushes or figs from thistles?"

Sadly there are many false prophets and so-called "Pastors" out there who would rather fleece the flock of God than feed the flock of God. They are very dangerous and divisive people who the child of God really needs to be wary of.

Unfortunately not every person who claims to be a Christian is genuine and not everyone who goes under the title of "Pastor" is being led by the Holy Spirit. I hope this poem can help us to determine the difference and encourage us to use our discernment before we let someone influence and lead us spiritually in life.

The tone of this poem isn't intended to be downcast and negative but rather my hope is that these words can be a positive influence overall. I pray the poem can encourage us to keep our eyes on Jesus and seek wisdom from His Throne.

Poem

Beware O' Christian the wolf in sheep's clothing,
He *may* know the Bible better than you.
He'll say "godly" things and pray with conviction;
He's learned the right lines and he knows what to do.

He'll play his role well, at least for a season.
He'll charm every soul with his silvery tongue,
Tricking God's people to follow intently,
With well applied Scriptures he'll fool everyone.

He'll mention God's name and claim to be humble,
Professing the life of one serving God's Throne
But listen more closely and hear his ambition;
The interests he's serving are purely his own.

Hear how he slanders and mocks other people,
Hear how he uses his words to destroy.
Beating the flock, condemning the brethren;
His sermons will leave you quite absent of joy.

Beware of his hunger for fame and for glory,
Dressing things up as his "Heavenly Call."
Christian be cautious when lending your talents;
You'll do all the work, *he'll* take credit for all.

Note how he focuses mainly on money,
Listing the ways you can loose the purse string.
He'll then buy support by controlling the wallet;
If you're deep in his pocket you can't confront him.

Treating the Church like his personal business,
Using God's people to gain his own wealth.
Slaying the saints as he climbs up the ladder,
Turning eyes *not* to Jesus but onto *himself.*

Beware O' Christian the wolf in sheep's clothing,
A godless persona is lurking beneath.
Given some time it *will* be seen clearly,
Behind the facade lies a predator's teeth.

Trust not his smile or words of approval,
Share not with him the depths of your heart.
Should you be found to thwart his agenda,
He'll turn on you quickly and tear you apart.

Though he may preach we should all be "united,"
Joined by our vision and sharing our goal,
He'll only unite with the ones who promote him;
The wolf will not stand those he cannot control.

So how does one spot a wolf in sheep's clothing?
Just look for the web of confusion he weaves.
You'll find in his wake division and sorrow,
The heartbreaking trail of destruction he leaves.

Bonds will be broken, ministries crippled,
Families fractured and friendships destroyed.
Ruthless he'll be in achieving his vision,
A wasteland will stand where his troops were deployed.

Only in Christ is there hope for his victims,
Take comfort O' Christian in God's sovereignty.
With eyes on the Lord we'll pick up the pieces
And *nothing* goes by that *His* eyes don't see!

The wolf cannot fool the God of creation,
His years of deception are already known.
Every performance must meet it's conclusion;
The masquerade over, he'll reap what he's sown.

But we dearest brethren, must use our discernment,
Praying for wisdom from Heaven above.
Childlike in faith yet sharp and insightful,
Wise as a serpent yet soft as a dove.

Listen O' Christian, the Shepherd is calling!
Hear how His voice has a *merciful* tone.
Flock to the side of our fearless Defender!
Our mighty Redeemer will lead us all home.

SCRIPTURE REFERENCES

Romans 16:17-18; 1 John 4:1; Matthew 10:16

NEW CREATION

I was at the gym one day when I got chatting to a lady next to me who told me her name was Mandy. She began to recommend a class that took place on a Sunday morning and so I thanked her for her suggestion but said that I wouldn't be able to make it as I go to Church on a Sunday. Mandy said straight away that she was searching for a deeper meaning to life and that she felt that something was definitely "missing." I replied, "At the risk of sounding crazy, you're right, there is something missing from your life. His name is Jesus and He loves you."

Mandy told me that she wanted to know more about Him and so we started going for a coffee after class each week and I shared the Gospel, some Christian booklets and a few of my poems with her. I was absolutely amazed to see how quickly the Holy Spirit started to work within Mandy's heart! I guess it's as the Bible says in Jeremiah 29:13,

"And you will seek Me and find Me, when you search for Me with all your heart."

After a few weeks of going to Church Mandy gave her heart to Jesus! I felt it was such an honour and a privilege that the Lord allowed me to be a part of her testimony and I'll always be so grateful for this experience.

When my Church organised a baptismal ceremony for August 2018 Mandy put her name down to take part. In the days leading up to the date I felt inspired to write a poem that I hoped would be a blessing not only to my dear friend but also to everyone being baptised that day. My prayer is that the poem might be able to be used by others too and shared at any baptism! Whenever numbers are added to the Body of Christ it certainly gives us a reason to celebrate!

POEM

Bless this day we pray O' Lord as we rejoice and sing;
You've added to the family of those who call You King!
Your Holy Spirit moved their soul and worked within their heart
So now we celebrate as their new life with Jesus starts!

Where condemnation stood we now find pardon in it's place,
We praise You for this miracle and thank you for Your grace!
Salvation is secured and every fear is washed away,
Eternal life is promised for Your love has won the day!

And so we come to witness their profession of this love
And pray Your many blessings flow upon them from above.
We know this act alone is not what saves us from our sin,
It's just the *outer* statement of the change that lies *within*.

Their soul already born-again and with a new direction,
Today we come to signify Your death and Resurrection.
The Cross has been acknowledged, repentance taken place
So now their life will always be secure in Your embrace!

A brand new child of God in whom the Saviour finds delight,
May joy be overflowing as our purposes unite!
We pray You give them courage and may their life inspire
Those who do not know You to fulfil their hearts' desire.

Help them find their strength in You, their strong and mighty Tower.
Teach them of Your goodness Lord and stun them with your power!
Help them learn to trust You as You lead them in Your way,
May they fall in love with Jesus more and more each day.

Let every care and burden now be brought before Your Throne
And when the trials come we pray they know they're not alone.
We ask You give *us* wisdom as we seek to help and guide.
May our fellowship be sweet, united as Your Bride.

We look towards the future with a hope and expectation
And long to see what fruit will come from this, Your new creation!
We join the hosts of Heaven as we sing in one accord;
Another soul is saved! Shout Hallelujah, praise the Lord!

SCRIPTURE REFERENCES

2 Corinthians 5:17; Mark 16:16; Luke 15:10; Isaiah 53:4-6

CHRISTMAS PRESENCE

INSPIRATION

In the lead up to Christmas 2018 I felt the Lord was showing me another side to the festive season. Illness within my family combined with watching friends go through various different trials made me aware that sometimes this can be a very difficult time of year for people.

There's also so much pressure put on us through television and adverts to have our lives live up to the "Christmas dream" and meet the "ideal image" of what Christmas time should be like. Scenes of carefree, happy families gathered around the table for a wonderful feast are projected from every screen for weeks leading up to Christmas Day! For so many reasons though this may not be the case for many people and this can lead to feelings such as depression, stress, inadequacy and isolation.

During this time I remember walking up towards Regent Street with my husband Jan one evening. We were going to see the incredible angels that light up that part of London at Christmas time. They normally bring so much joy and excitement to my heart but after a bad diagnosis from the doctor was given to someone very close to me I found myself remarking to Jan,

"I'm looking at all the same, amazing twinkling lights as yesterday but now they've completely lost their sparkle for me."

By God's grace and mercy, Christmas 2018 was still a wonderful one in spite of the challenges we faced. His incredible ability to heal had my family singing His praises on Christmas Eve! I felt inspired to write a poem however that might address this subject and hopefully bring comfort and encouragement to someone who may not be feeling the festive spirit like everyone else around them seems to be.

If you feel the festive lights have lost their appealing twinkle or you're facing this Christmas with a heavy heart, I pray this poem can bring the focus back onto the real meaning of Christmas and encourage your soul today. In the midst of all the glitter and the bustle of the season, let's remember the miracle of that first Christmas when God humbled Himself and came in the form of Man. Well are the words sung each year,

"Veiled in flesh the Godhead see, hail the incarnate Deity!"

No matter what's going on in your life today remember you have a Saviour. I pray that you'd be filled with His peace and enveloped by His loving presence as you draw close to Him this Christmas.

POEM

Christmas can be wonderful, a special time of year.
A time when many hearts and homes are filled with festive cheer.
Oh what joy to hear the songs and see the twinkling lights
As thrilling Christmas sights and smells bring warmth to winter nights.

Yet Christmas can be difficult and though it's set apart,
For some it is a time endured and with a heavy heart.
Nostalgic thoughts or deep regrets bring feelings of despair,
Or facing Christmas dinner with a newly empty chair.

Financial woes and illnesses care not for Christmas peace.
Some trials are relentless and never seem to cease.
Though yuletide hymns may fill the air, bringing joy and glee,
For some they highlight just how lonely Christmas time can be.

Yet through our tribulation we know we can take heart
For One has overcome this world and set our lives apart.
The Baby in the manger was sent from God above.
In Him alone we find our hope, our peace, our joy, our love.

These things we can receive through Christ for God is generous.
A precious list of Christmas gifts our Saviour gives to us.
Although we may be downcast we needn't be forlorn,
Remembering that Christmas is the time when Hope was born!

Hope that pierced the darkness to save the souls of man,
Redemption set in place by God before the world began.
Our hope through tribulation, though it may seem absurd
Is rooted in the certainty and promise of God's Word.

Each morning brings new mercies, His compassions never fail.
Abounding in our hope through Christ we know we can prevail!
Hope for life eternal prevents us giving in
For Jesus is our portion and there's always hope in Him.

This precious gift He gives us allays our fear and doubt,
Christ's hope within our hearts is like a flame that won't go out.
It's presence ever faithful will bring the soul a lift.
When hope in God has been embraced then comes the second gift.

Peace that overflows within and brings our spirit rest
For Jesus took our sins as far as East is from the West!
Peace in God's forgiveness, to know our debt is paid
So let your heart be troubled not nor let it be afraid.

Justified by faith in Christ, united with our King;
Tranquility and righteousness that only He can bring!
Although we may be troubled we needn't be forlorn,
Remembering that Christmas is the time when Peace was born.

Sent to us from Heaven to fulfil the Father's plan,
The Catalyst through whom would come the peace for God and man.
Now we know the richness of God's sweet communication,
Praise to the Almighty! There is peace for every nation!

Purchased by the blood of Christ, released from guilt and shame,
Accepted through His sacrifice we praise His holy name!
God struck the heart of darkness through His precious baby Boy,
When peace with Him has been embraced then comes the gift of joy!

Joy in our Redeemer, knowing He is in control.
Joy that grows in heart and mind and infiltrates the soul!
Joy that's not reliant upon any circumstance,
Joy that glows and radiates through shining countenance!

Though "happiness" be fickle and a fleeting state of mind,
Joy remains through hardship for at it's roots we find
The God who made the moon and stars and gave the breath of life,
Gives constant strength and help to those who suffer times of strife.

Although we may be weary we needn't be forlorn,
Remembering that Christmas is the time when Joy was born.
Only through this Saviour can our spirit grow and flourish
And tragedy is often where our faith is deeply nourished.

His joy will cast away our fears and fill our heart with reverence,
Joy that's overflowing when we rest in Jesus' presence.
Joy that stirs an inner song to hail our God above.
When joy in Christ has been embraced then comes the gift of love!

Love for other people, love for fellow man,
Inspired by the Prince of Peace, our God, the great I Am!
Although we may be broken we needn't be forlorn,
Remembering that Christmas is the time when Love was born!

Though draped in Heaven's glories, Christ chose to leave His Throne!
In human flesh He came to have the Father's love made known.
The Lord of Earth and Heaven was willing to descend,
Burdened by humanity, He died and rose again!

The God of new beginnings makes broken spirits whole,
The God who breathes new life into the dead parts of the soul!
Endless love through Jesus who wipes away each tear.
His love, the perfect present to unwrap this time of year!

Let us not be mournful, let not our spirits sigh
For Christmas is the time when God responded to our cry.
Behold! The door is open for healing and salvation,
Redemption and eternal life await for every nation!

Glory in the highest! Let our sorrows melt away
As we offer up our praises and exalt His name today!
May the love of Jesus enfold us this Noel.
The victory is won through Him, our God, Emmanuel!

This Christmas may we bask in Christ, our Gift from God above
And dwell in sweet surrender and the safety of His love.
May this season bring new joy and fill us with a reverence
For Jesus Christ our Saviour and His awesome Christmas Presence.

Scripture Referneces

Matthew 11:28; Isaiah 40:31; Lamentations 3:22-26; John 16:33;
Philippians 4:6-7; Nehemiah 8:10; Romans 15:13; John 3:16;
1 John 3:1; 1 Peter 5:6-7

CHOOSE THIS DAY

INSPIRATION

I received an e-mail one day from a dear Christian lady called Wendy, asking if I would pray for a friend of hers who was slipping away from life and didn't know Jesus as her Saviour. I joined Wendy in praying for her friend and found myself asking the Lord to bring someone along who might minister to the woman in her last days.

The next day Wendy asked me if I had any poetry verses that may speak to her friend at that time. Immediately the first few verses from my poem "Wave Upon The Sand" came to mind and I sent them along to her but the thought came to me that it would be beneficial to have a poem that was specifically written for this kind of situation.

Straight away I heard the words "Choose This Day" along with seeing a picture in my mind of a person sitting by the bedside of a loved one, reading a poem and sharing Jesus. I said to my husband Jan that I felt I needed to write a poem that could be used by Christians to bring the Gospel to those who are facing their mortality and don't know Jesus as their personal Saviour.

I wrote this poem in three hours from start to finish that very same evening and sent it along to Wendy right away. I was very aware as I was writing that I wanted to find a balance where the words and tone would be very sensitive to what is undoubtedly an emotional and upsetting situation yet deliver the fullness of the Gospel in love and truth without apology. I feel that in moments like this there's nothing left to lose.

My prayer for this poem is that it may be used as a powerful tool by many to reach the souls of the lost before it's too late. The thought of looking into eternity without Jesus is beyond words. When a soul is at stake I feel the most important thing a person can share is the love of God and make known the forgiveness, peace and salvation that's available to us through His Son Jesus Christ. A few minutes of discomfort in this life is more than worth it for the sake of eternal life with Him.

I've added an example of the "sinner's prayer" to the end of this poem in case an opportunity comes up to lead another to Christ in prayer. I pray the poem and the prayer may be used many times over!

Poem

Dear one I come before you with a burden on my heart,
I wish to share the truth before the time comes to depart.
I pray do not be angry for in love I've come to speak,
I only want the best for you and this is what I seek.

With all that is within me I now must plead my case,
I wish to share the Gospel and reveal to you God's grace.
May your ears be opened up to hear your Maker's voice,
The end is drawing near and so you have to make your choice.

Created in His image, He formed your very heart.
Unique beyond all measure, you're His precious work of art!
Your Maker gifted you with life for purposes divine,
The days you have appointed are by Heavenly design.

But sullied by rebellion, we all must face the truth
That sin has played a mighty role, our fallen ways are proof.
None can claim perfection and though the truth is stark,
We have to face the fact that all mankind has missed the mark.

Dear one do not be fearful though, do not be at a loss!
Redemption can be yours through Jesus' work upon the Cross!
Every fault and failure, every single sin
Was nailed upon the Tree with Christ and paid in full by Him.

He bought eternal freedom and took away your shame,
He gifts you with Salvation by just trusting in His name!
If tempted to look back on life, you needn't feel regret.
Your Saviour loves you dearly so He cleared your every debt.

Think not of your misgivings, dwell not on your mistakes.
Trust in Jesus' sacrifice for this is all it takes.
The Saviour took your punishment and paid for every sin,
Salvation's there to claim but you must give your heart to Him.

Trust not in your achievements, rest not in man's acclaim.
Eternal life awaits for those who call upon His name.
I share with you the knowledge that good works will not suffice.
No matter what you've done you need to put your faith in Christ.

Enter through the narrow gate and reap His great reward.
Run into the loving arms of Jesus Christ our Lord!
He's waited for you patiently and calls you faithfully.
Open up your heart to Him and choose to bow the knee.

No judgement will you face for His payment has sufficed,
No condemnation can be found for those secure in Christ.
Dear one it's up to you on which eternity you choose,
You've everything to gain and not a single thing to lose!

Respond this day to Jesus, He's the Author of your story,
Awaken to His wonders as you enter into glory!
May you seize this moment to know His peace I pray.
Choose your Saviour dearest one, choose your God this day.

SCRIPTURE REFERENCES

Joshua 24:15; Joel 2:32; Psalm 145:18; Matthew 7:13-14; Romans 8:1

THE SINNER'S PRAYER

Heavenly Father, I come to you in prayer asking for the forgiveness of my sins. I believe in my heart that Jesus Christ is Your Son and that He died on the Cross in my place and rose again. I believe that His sacrifice paid the penalty for my sins so that I might be forgiven and have eternal life in the Kingdom of Heaven. I am willing to turn from my sin and ask You right now to come into my life and be my personal Saviour and Lord. I commit myself to You and ask You to send the Holy Spirit into my heart to fill me. I confess with my mouth and in my heart that I am born again and cleansed by the blood of Jesus. All that I am I now commit into Your hands. Thank You Father for loving me, in Jesus' name I pray. Amen.

POETRY CATEGORIES

TESTIMONY

BEING SINGLE, MARRIAGE, LOVE

GOSPEL, WORK OF THE CROSS

TRIALS

PHYSICAL PAIN

CHILDREN

RELIGIOUS MISCONCEPTIONS

EVANGELISM

COMMITMENT

PERSECUTION

POLITICS

CHRISTMAS, NEW YEAR

SUFFERING

END TIMES

GRACE, FORGIVENESS